Soups and Breads

The Confident Cooking Promise of Success

Welcome to the world of Confident Cooking,
where recipes are double-tested by our team
of home economists to achieve a high standard
of success—and delicious results every time.

bay books

CONTENTS

Watercress and potato soup, page 27

Pumpkin damper, page 91

Saffron and mussel soup, page 60

Vegetable and watercress soup, page 16

Cream of mushroom soup, page 70

Rich oxtail soup, page 23

The Publisher thanks the following for their assistance: Sunbeam Corporation Ltd; Kambrook; Waterford Wedgwood; Villeroy & Boch

White dinner rolls, page 90

Hot beef borscht, page 48

All recipes are double-tested by our team of home economists. When we test our recipes, we rate them for ease of preparation. The following cookery ratings are on the recipes in this book, making them easy to use and understand.

A single Cooking with Confidence symbol indicates a recipe that is simple and generally quick to make —perfect for beginners.

Two symbols indicate the need for just a little more care and a little more time.

Three symbols indicate special dishes that need more investment in time, care and patience—but the results are worth it.

IMPORTANT
Those who might be at risk from the effects of salmonella food poisoning (the elderly, pregnant women, young children and those suffering from immune deficiency diseases) should consult their doctor with any concerns about eating raw eggs.

Easy soups and breads

There's nothing quite like home-made soup, served piping hot with warm-from-the-oven bread. Both are enjoyable and surprisingly easy to make if you follow a few commonsense rules, and can be dressed up or down to suit just about any occasion.

The French quotation states 'soup is to dinner what the gateway is to a building', meaning that the soup should be chosen carefully to lead the diners into the meal. With some soups, such as consommés and light broths, this is still the case, but many others have become delicious, nutritious, flavour-packed meals in their own right. Today there are many different types of soup, varying in preparation, creaminess and consistency. We have broths, chowders, bouillons, consommés, as well as all manner of creamy soups.

The story goes that the most famous soup of all, Minestrone, was first tasted during the Crusades when Italian soldiers boiled up meat in water to make a simple broth, then asked the neighbouring villagers to contribute vegetables and herbs. Such humble beginnings for one of the world's most popular dishes.

STOCK SECRETS

While soup is the ideal vehicle for using up odds and ends from the refrigerator, it is only as good as its ingredients, and the backbone of any good soup is its stock. There are several alternatives when choosing stock. You can use home-made (see page 82), fresh or frozen stock available from some delicatessens or poultry shops, or tetra packs or cubes from the supermarket. The best stock will be home-made or fresh and, as it can be frozen, it is a good idea to cook up large quantities every time. Tetra packs are convenient, as are stock cubes; however, check the labels and choose cubes made from natural ingredients with no added MSG. Commercial stocks always tend to be much saltier than home-made, so taste the soup before seasoning with salt and pepper. Always season soup at the end of the cooking time, as long cooking concentrates the flavours.

Try to use the flavour stock called for in the recipe. A beef stock would be overpowering in a recipe that calls for chicken stock, although vegetarians might prefer to use vegetable stock in all their soups.

PUREEING AND STRAINING

Many soups are puréed before serving and there is a sensible way to go about this. Let the soup cool a little first, so that it is safe if it splashes. Cool it quickly by pouring it into a bowl, then wash the pan to take the puréed soup for reheating. Purée in either a food processor or a blender—a blender will give a finer result, though it tends to aerate the soup slightly. Always purée in batches, never filling the processor above halfway.

SIMMERING SOUPS

Most recipes call for a heavy-based pan for making soup. This is so that the pan distributes heat evenly and prevents anything 'catching' on the bottom. A wide, shallow pan will allow too much evaporation. The recipe will state if the pan should be covered. If it is not to be covered the soup will simmer and, as the liquid evaporates off it, it will reduce down and thicken. So, if your soup is still a little thin, simply simmer it uncovered for a while. Most soups are cooked at a gentle simmer, meaning that the surface of the soup is barely moving, while a simmer means the soup will be moving faster but without bubbles breaking the surface. Boiling is when bubbles actively break the surface of the soup. Watch the soup and adjust the heat accordingly. If the recipe says to partially cover the pan, tilt the lid at an angle so that there is a gap for steam to escape.

The surface of a simmering soup moves quite quickly.

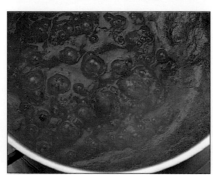

Bubbles will be breaking on the surface when the soup is boiling.

Tilt the lid at an angle if the recipe calls for a partially covered pan.

Occasionally, recipes ask for the soup to be strained, particularly if making the stock is part of the recipe. A fine sieve (not a colander) is usually adequate. Some clear soups need more than one straining, through a sieve lined with damp muslin. If you don't have muslin, use a clean damp chux (kitchen cloth).

Clear soups can be strained through a sieve lined with damp muslin.

AHEAD OF TIME

Many soups can be made in advance and do, in fact, benefit from overnight refrigeration as the flavours develop. Use commonsense to determine if any of the ingredients will not store well, for example if the soup has cream, add it when you are reheating for serving. The same goes for pasta; for instance, if you add the pasta to Minestrone, then leave it to sit around, it will be unpleasantly soggy. Generally, soups can be kept for up to 3 days in the refrigerator, or frozen in airtight containers or freezer bags for up to 1–3 months. A lot of soups become very thick on standing and need to be diluted when reheated. Use more of the same stock, water or cream, as appropriate. The seasoning will also need to be adjusted.

Some soups thicken on standing and need to be diluted when they are reheated.

BREAD

This book gives recipes for quickbreads, such as muffins and damper, as well as yeast-raised loaves. These take a little more time, most of which is unattended, but with a bit of planning are just as easy.

You will find it useful to have an understanding of some of the elements of bread-making before you begin. Yeast is probably the most important ingredient and is available either dried or fresh. Dried yeast generally comes in a box containing 7 g (1/4 oz) sachets, one of which is enough for a standard loaf, and is available from supermarkets. Fresh yeast is sold in blocks, from health food stores or delicatessens, and is kept refrigerated. It is sometimes difficult to buy, and has a short shelf life. Both forms of yeast are interchangeable; substitute 15 g (1/2 oz) of fresh yeast for 7 g (1/4 oz) of dried. If you don't have kitchen scales, a level tablespoon of firmly packed fresh yeast weighs 15 g , while a teaspoon of dried weighs 3 g.

The first step is usually to dissolve the yeast in warm liquid ingredients (usually water and milk). This is then left in a warm place for about 10 minutes. It should become frothy and increase in volume; if it doesn't, it means the yeast is not active and should be discarded. This mixture is then added to the dry ingredients and mixed to a soft dough. The dough is then formed into a ball on a lightly floured surface and kneaded. Don't be tempted to cut short the kneading time, as it affects the texture of the finished bread. The action is simple— stretch the dough by pushing it away from you with the heel of your hand, fold back and make a quarter turn. Get into the rhythm and when you are finished the dough should be smooth and elastic. Don't overwork it or it will be tough.

Place the dough in an oiled bowl covered with greased plastic wrap and leave it in a warm, draught-free spot to 'prove' (rise), until doubled in size. The warmth helps the dough to rise but too much heat can interfere with the yeast action. If the temperature is cool, it will take longer for the dough to rise, but this will not have any adverse effect on the bread.

After proving, 'punch down' the dough (literally—one punch) to expel the air, and knead again briefly. The dough is now ready to shape.

These instructions are general, and should be used in conjunction with the individual recipes, as particular ingredients in the breads may require different treatment.

Home-made bread doesn't keep as long as shop-bought, as it contains no preservatives. It's best eaten the day it is made, or toasted the next day. It can be frozen, in a bag with all the air squeezed out, for up to 3 months. Thaw it at room temperature and 'refresh' in a moderate 180°C (350°F/ Gas 4) oven for about 10 minutes.

To knead, push the dough away from you with the heel of your hand.

Put the dough in an oiled bowl and cover with greased plastic wrap.

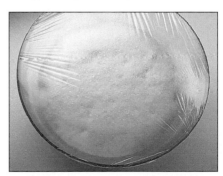

Leave in a warm place until the dough has doubled in size.

SOUPS

BOUILLABAISSE

Preparation time: 40 minutes
Total cooking time: 1 hour 20 minutes
Serves 4–6

4–6 tomatoes
500 g (1 lb) raw king prawns
1 raw lobster tail
1–2 fish heads
1 cup (250 ml/8 fl oz) red wine
3 onions, finely chopped
6 cloves garlic, crushed
3 bay leaves
¼ cup (60 ml/2 fl oz) olive oil
1 leek, finely sliced
¼ cup (60 g/2 oz) tomato paste
small piece of orange rind
500 g (1 lb) white fish fillet,
    cut into small pieces
12 mussels, firmly closed,
    scrubbed and beards
    removed
200 g (6½ oz) scallops with
    corals
½ cup (30 g/1 oz) chopped
    parsley
¼ cup (15 g/½ oz) shredded
    basil leaves

1 Score a cross in the base of each tomato. Cover with boiling water for 1 minute, plunge in cold water, drain and peel away the skins.
2 To make the fish stock, peel and devein the prawns and set the shells, heads and tails aside. Shell the lobster tail, keeping the shell and chopping the meat. Put the lobster shell, fish heads, prawn shells, heads and tails in a large pan. Add the wine, 1 onion, 2 cloves garlic, 1 bay leaf and 2 cups (500 ml/16 fl oz) of water. Bring to the boil, reduce the heat and simmer for 20 minutes. Strain through a fine sieve, reserving the stock.
3 Heat the oil in a large, heavy-based pan. Add the leek and remaining onion and garlic. Cover and simmer, stirring occasionally, over low heat for 20 minutes, or until browned. Add the tomato, remaining bay leaves, tomato paste and orange rind and stir well. Remove the lid and continue to cook for 10 minutes, stirring occasionally. Add the reserved fish stock, bring to the boil, reduce the heat and simmer for 10 minutes, stirring occasionally.
4 Add the prawns, lobster, fish pieces, mussels and scallops. Simmer, covered, for 4–5 minutes. Discard any unopened mussels, the rind and bay leaves. Add the herbs and season to taste with salt and freshly ground black pepper. The Bouillabaisse is shown here with a bowlful of Rouille (page 52), a delicious accompaniment.

NUTRITION PER SERVE (6)
Protein 45 g; Fat 30 g; Carbohydrate 15 g; Dietary Fibre 6 g; Cholesterol 185 mg; 2165 kJ (520 cal)

Cut on either side of the soft underside of the lobster tail, and lift up.

Strain through a fine sieve, reserving the stock.

POTATO AND CHEESE SOUP

Preparation time: 20 minutes
Total cooking time: 40 minutes
Serves 4–6

30 g (1 oz) butter
4 rashers bacon, cut into strips
1 onion, finely chopped
1/2 teaspoon sweet paprika
1 kg (2 lb) potatoes, chopped
3 cups (750 ml/24 fl oz) chicken
    stock (see page 82)
1 cup (125 g/4 oz) grated
    Cheddar
chopped chives, to serve

1 Melt the butter in a large pan, add the bacon and cook until crisp. Remove the bacon from the pan with a slotted spoon, leaving as much fat as possible. Add the onion to the same pan and cook for 5 minutes, or until very soft and golden. Add the paprika and cook for a further 30 seconds.
2 Return the bacon to the pan and add the potato and stock. Bring to the boil, then reduce the heat and simmer for 30 minutes, or until the potato is very soft. Stir or mash lightly to break up the potato. Add the Cheddar and stir well, until it is melted through. Season with salt and pepper to taste and serve topped with a sprinkling of chopped chives.

NUTRITION PER SERVE (6)
Protein 15 g; Fat 15 g; Carbohydrate 25 g; Dietary Fibre 3 g; Cholesterol 50 mg; 1120 kJ (270 cal)

COOK'S FILE

Serving suggestion: This soup goes very well with the Tomato herb rolls on page 105.

Trim the rind and excess fat from the bacon and cut into strips.

Cook the bacon until crisp and remove from the pan with a slotted spoon.

Stir with a wooden spoon or mash lightly to break up the potato.

MOROCCAN CHICKPEA SOUP

Preparation time: 35 minutes
  + overnight soaking
Total cooking time: 1 hour 10 minutes
Serves 4

250 g (8 oz) dried chickpeas
2 tablespoons olive oil
1 onion, finely sliced
2 teaspoons ground cumin
2 teaspoons sweet paprika
1 teaspoon ground ginger
1 teaspoon ground cinnamon
1/4 teaspoon allspice

250 g (8 oz) boneless lamb leg
  steaks, cut into strips
500 g (1 lb) tomatoes, finely
  chopped
8 cups (2 litres) vegetable stock
  or water (see page 82)
2 teaspoons grated lemon rind
1/2 cup (110 g/3 1/2 oz) short-
  grain rice
1/4 cup (7 g/1/4 oz) chopped
  parsley
2 tablespoons chopped
  coriander

1 Soak the chickpeas in cold water overnight. Drain. Heat the oil in a large pan over low heat and add the onion and spices. Cook for 15 minutes, covered, stirring occasionally.

2 Add the chickpeas, lamb, tomato and stock. Bring to the boil, reduce the heat and simmer for 35 minutes. Skim the surface as required. Add the lemon rind and rice and cook for 12 minutes, or until the rice is tender. Add the herbs and season to taste.

NUTRITION PER SERVE
Protein 30 g; Fat 15 g; Carbohydrate 45 g;
Dietary Fibre 10 g; Cholesterol 40 mg;
1760 kJ (420 cal)

COOK'S FILE

Note: Short-grain rice is plump and sticks together when cooked.

Soak the chickpeas in plenty of cold water and leave overnight. Drain well.

Use a sharp knife to cut the lamb leg steaks into strips.

Add the onion, cumin, paprika, ginger, cinnamon and allspice to the pan.

CREAMY SPINACH AND CHICKEN SOUP

Preparation time: 40 minutes
Total cooking time: 55 minutes
Serves 6

1 tablespoon oil
1 kg (2 lb) chicken pieces
1 carrot, chopped
2 celery sticks, chopped
1 onion, chopped
6 black peppercorns
2 cloves garlic, chopped
1 bouquet garni

800 g (1 lb 10 oz) white sweet
   potato, chopped
2 bunches (about 500 g/1 lb)
   English spinach
½ cup (125 ml/4 fl oz) cream

1 Heat the oil in a large pan, add the chicken in batches and brown well. Drain on paper towels. Pour off the excess fat, leaving 1 tablespoon in the pan. Return the chicken to the pan with the carrot, celery, onion, peppercorns, garlic, bouquet garni and 6 cups (1.5 litres) of water. Bring to the boil, reduce the heat and simmer for 40 minutes. Strain, returning the

stock to the pan. Pull the chicken meat from the bones, shred and set aside.
2 Add the sweet potato to the stock in the pan. Bring to the boil, reduce the heat and simmer until tender. Add the spinach leaves and cook until wilted. Process in batches in a food processor until finely chopped.
3 Return to the pan, add the chicken and stir in the cream. Season to taste. Reheat gently before serving but do not allow the soup to boil.

NUTRITION PER SERVE
Protein 40 g; Fat 15 g; Carbohydrate 25 g; Dietary Fibre 4 g; Cholesterol 110 mg; 1720 kJ (410 cal)

To make a bouquet garni, tie parsley, thyme and a bay leaf with string.

Brown the chicken in batches then drain on paper towels.

Add the spinach leaves to the soup and cook, stirring, until just wilted.

FRENCH ONION SOUP

Preparation time: 15 minutes
Total cooking time: 1 hour 30 minutes
Serves 4–6

1 tablespoon olive oil
30 g (1 oz) butter
1 kg (2 lb) onions, thinly sliced
1½ tablespoons soft brown
 sugar
4 tablespoons plain flour
6 cups (1.5 litres) beef stock
 (see page 82)
½ cup (125 ml/4 fl oz) brandy
¼ cup (60 ml/2 fl oz) olive oil,
 extra
2 cloves garlic, crushed
1 French bread stick
1 cup (100 g/3½ oz) grated
 Parmesan

1 Heat the oil and butter in a large, heavy-based pan. Add the onion and stir over low heat for 1 minute. Cover and cook for a further 20 minutes, stirring occasionally. Add the sugar and ½ teaspoon of salt and increase the heat. Cook for 30 minutes, stirring frequently, or until the onion is golden brown.
2 Gradually add the flour. Cook for 3 minutes over medium heat, stirring. Remove from the heat and gradually add the combined stock and brandy.
3 Over medium heat, bring to the boil, stirring constantly, until slightly thickened. Partially cover the saucepan, lower the heat and simmer gently for 30 minutes, stirring occasionally. Season to taste.
4 Mix the extra oil and garlic. Cut the bread stick into thick slices and toast both sides under a preheated grill, until lightly browned. Brush on the oil

and sprinkle with the Parmesan. Grill until melted and serve on the soup.

NUTRITION PER SERVE (6)
Protein 15 g; Fat 25 g; Carbohydrate 30 g; Dietary Fibre 4 g; Cholesterol 30 mg; 1800 kJ (430 cal)

COOK'S FILE

Note: Although it is more expensive, you can use Reggiano Parmesan for this recipe; it has an excellent creamy taste and rich, grainy texture. It is available from delicatessens.

Cook the onion, stirring frequently, until it is a rich golden brown.

Stirring with a wooden spoon, gradually add the combined stock and brandy.

Using a pastry brush, coat one side of the toast with the oil mixture.

WON TON SOUP

Preparation time: 50 minutes
+ 30 minutes soaking
Total cooking time: 40 minutes
Serves 4

2 dried Chinese mushrooms
15 raw prawns
100 g (3½ oz) pork mince
2 spring onions, chopped
1 teaspoon grated ginger
2 tablespoons canned water
    chestnuts, chopped
2 teaspoons chopped lemon
    grass, white part only
1 clove garlic, finely chopped

3 tablespoons soy sauce
225 g (7 oz) won ton
    wrappers
coriander leaves
6 cups (1.5 litres) beef stock
    (see page 82)
3 baby carrots, cut diagonally
3 spring onions, cut diagonally

1 Soak the mushrooms in hot water for 30 minutes. Peel and devein the prawns, then cut in half lengthways. Drain the mushrooms, remove the stems and chop the caps.
2 Mix the chopped mushroom with the pork, spring onion, ginger, water chestnut, lemon grass, garlic and 1 tablespoon of the soy sauce. Work

with 1 won ton wrapper at a time, keeping the rest covered. Put 2–3 coriander leaves, half a prawn and a heaped teaspoon of the pork mixture in the centre of a wrapper. Brush the edges with water and lay another wrapper on top. Press to seal. Repeat with the remaining wrappers.
3 Bring the stock, remaining soy sauce, carrot and spring onion to the boil. Bring another large pan of water to the boil and cook the won tons in batches for 4–5 minutes; drain. Pour the hot soup over the won tons.

NUTRITION PER SERVE
Protein 20 g; Fat 4 g; Carbohydrate 50 g; Dietary Fibre 5 g; Cholesterol 90 mg; 1290 kJ (310 cal)

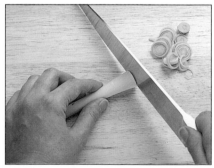

Thinly slice the white part of the lemon grass, then chop finely.

Remove the stems from the soaked mushrooms and finely chop the caps.

Lightly brush the edges with a little water, then lay another wrapper on top.

CREAM OF TOMATO SOUP

Preparation time: 25 minutes
Total cooking time: 30 minutes
Serves 4

1.25 kg (2½ lb) tomatoes
1 tablespoon oil
1 onion, chopped
1 clove garlic, chopped
1½ cups (375 ml/12 fl oz)
    chicken stock
    (see page 82)
2 tablespoons tomato paste
1 teaspoon sugar
1 cup (250 ml/8 fl oz) cream

1 Cut a cross in the base of each tomato. Cover with boiling water for 1 minute, plunge in iced water, drain and peel away the skins. Scoop out the seeds and discard, then roughly chop the flesh.

2 Heat the oil in a large pan and cook the onion for 3 minutes, or until soft. Add the garlic and cook for 1 minute longer. Add the tomato and cook for 5 minutes, stirring occasionally, until very soft. Stir in the stock, bring to the boil, reduce the heat and simmer for 10 minutes.

3 Cool slightly, then transfer to a food processor. Process in batches until smooth, and return to the pan. Add the tomato paste and sugar and

bring to the boil, stirring continuously. Reduce the heat and stir in the cream but do not allow the soup to boil. Season to taste before serving. Serve with an extra spoonful of cream and chopped parsley, if you want.

NUTRITION PER SERVE
Protein 5 g; Fat 30 g; Carbohydrate 10 g; Dietary Fibre 5 g; Cholesterol 85 mg; 1480 kJ (350 cal)

COOK'S FILE

Hint: It is best to use plump, ripe tomatoes for this recipe.
Note: If you are not using home-made stock, remember to taste the soup before seasoning. Shop-bought stock can be very salty.

Plunge the tomatoes into iced water, then peel away the skin.

Cook, stirring with a wooden spoon, until the tomato is very soft.

Add the tomato paste and sugar and bring to the boil, stirring until smooth.

FENNEL, ASPARAGUS AND PEA SOUP

Preparation time: 20 minutes
Total cooking time: 40 minutes
Serves 4

30 g (1 oz) butter
1½ tablespoons olive oil
1 leek, white part only, sliced
1 fennel bulb, sliced
375 g (12 oz) asparagus, cut
    into pieces
1 clove garlic, crushed
8 mint leaves, chopped
150 g (5 oz) shelled or frozen
    peas (400 g/13 oz in pods)
200 g (6½ oz) potatoes, cubed
4 cups (1 litre) chicken or
    vegetable stock (see page 83)
pinch of cayenne pepper
pinch of ground nutmeg

Mint and garlic croutons
20 g (¾ oz) butter
1 tablespoon olive oil
2 slices day-old white bread,
    crusts removed, cut into four
mint leaves
2 cloves garlic, sliced, soaked in
    cold water for 15 minutes

1 Heat the butter and oil in a large pan and add the leek and fennel. Cook over medium heat for 8–10 minutes, then stir in the asparagus, garlic, mint, peas and potato. Cook for 1 minute longer.
2 Add enough stock to cover the vegetables, and bring to the boil. Remove 4 asparagus tips, plunge into a bowl of iced water and set aside. Reduce the heat and simmer for 15–20 minutes, or until the vegetables are tender. Cool slightly then purée in a food processor. Return to the pan with the remaining stock, cayenne pepper and nutmeg and season.
3 Preheat the oven to moderately hot 190°C (375°F/Gas 5). To make the croutons, melt the butter and oil and brush on both sides of the bread. Lay on a baking tray. Tear the mint leaves in half, and place on the bread; dry the garlic and place on the mint. Drizzle the remaining butter mixture over the top. Bake for 5–6 minutes, or until the bread is toasted and the garlic golden.
4 Gently reheat the soup and serve garnished with the croutons and the reserved asparagus tips.

NUTRITION PER SERVE
Protein 15 g; Fat 25 g; Carbohydrate 30 g; Dietary Fibre 10 g; Cholesterol 30 mg; 1570 kJ (375 cal)

Split the pods to remove the peas; or string the pod by pulling from the top.

Using tongs, remove 4 asparagus tips and plunge into iced water.

Lay the mint leaves and garlic slices on the bread.

CHICKPEA, CHORIZO AND PORK RIB SOUP

Preparation time: 20 minutes
 + overnight soaking
Total cooking time: 40 minutes
Serves 6–8

180 g (6 oz) dried chickpeas
300 g (10 oz) smoked bacon
  ribs
2 tablespoons olive oil
1 onion, finely chopped
1 clove garlic, crushed
2 tomatoes, peeled, seeded and
  finely chopped
1 potato, cubed

1 carrot, sliced
200 g (6½ oz) pumpkin,
  chopped
150 g (5 oz) chorizo or
  pepperoni sausage, sliced
¼ teaspoon dried oregano
6 cups (1.5 litres) chicken stock
  (see page 82)

1 Soak the chickpeas in cold water overnight. Drain.
2 Blanch the bacon ribs in boiling water for 30 seconds, then plunge into iced water. Drain and slice into pieces.
3 Heat the oil in a large, heavy-based pan and cook the onion over medium heat for 3–4 minutes, stirring continuously. Add the garlic and

tomato and cook for a further 5 minutes.
4 Add the chickpeas, ribs, potato, carrot, pumpkin, chorizo, dried oregano and stock. Bring to the boil, then reduce the heat and simmer, covered, for 30 minutes, or until the chickpeas are tender. Season to taste.

NUTRITION PER SERVE (8)
Protein 15 g; Fat 15 g; Carbohydrate 15 g; Dietary Fibre 4 g; Cholesterol 30 mg; 1110 kJ (240 cal)

COOK'S FILE

Note: If bacon ribs are unavailable, use 150 g (5 oz) smoked bacon instead.
Serving suggestion: Serve with Roasted red capsicum buns, page 100.

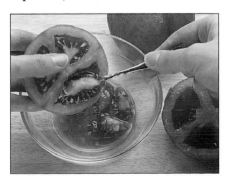
Halve the peeled tomatoes and scoop out the seeds using a teaspoon.

Use chorizo, pepperoni or another type of spicy sausage.

Drain the blanched ribs, then cut into smaller sections.

VEGETABLE AND WATERCRESS SOUP

Preparation time: 40 minutes
Total cooking time: 1 hour
Serves 4

1 kg (2 lb) chicken bones
8 cm (3 inch) piece of ginger, roughly chopped
several celery leaves
2 carrots, roughly chopped
6 spring onions, roughly chopped
2 carrots, extra
2 sticks celery
2 leeks
200 g (6½ oz) whole baby corn
1 head broccoli
50 g (1¾ oz) baby beans or whole beans cut into short lengths
100 g (3½ oz) sugar snap peas
2–3 tablespoons soy sauce
1–2 tablespoons sesame oil
2 cups (60 g/2 oz) watercress sprigs, to serve

1 To make the chicken stock, place the chicken bones, ginger, celery leaves, chopped carrot, spring onion and a teaspoon of salt in a large pan. Cover with 8 cups (2 litres) of water and bring to the boil. Reduce the heat to low and simmer for 45 minutes, skimming the surface as required.

2 Cut the extra carrots and celery into matchsticks and the leeks into strips. Cut the corn in half lengthways and trim the broccoli into florets.

3 Strain the stock and discard the bones and vegetables. Strain again through a very fine sieve and bring the stock to a simmer. Add the carrot, corn and baby beans and cook for 3 minutes. Add the celery, leek, broccoli and sugar snap peas and cook for a further 3–4 minutes. Do not overcook the vegetables: they should be tender but crisp.

4 Add the soy sauce and sesame oil and season to taste with salt and pepper. Add the watercress and serve immediately with some extra sesame oil and soy sauce, if you want.

NUTRITION PER SERVE
Protein 9 g; Fat 6 g; Carbohydrate 25 g; Dietary Fibre 10 g; Cholesterol 0 mg; 800 kJ (200 cal)

Trim the coarse stems from the watercress.

Cut the carrots and celery into matchsticks, and the leeks into strips.

Using a sharp knife, cut the broccoli into small florets.

Strain the stock a second time through a fine sieve.

MANHATTAN-STYLE SEAFOOD CHOWDER

Preparation time: 30 minutes
Total cooking time: 30 minutes
Serves 4–6

60 g (2 oz) butter
3 rashers bacon, chopped
2 onions, chopped
2 cloves garlic, finely chopped
2 sticks celery, sliced
3 potatoes, diced
5 cups (1.25 litres) fish or
chicken stock (see page 82)
3 teaspoons chopped thyme

1 tablespoon tomato paste
425 g (14 oz) can chopped
tomatoes
375 g (12 oz) boneless white
fish fillets, cut into chunks
12 large raw prawns, peeled,
deveined and halved
310 g (10 oz) can baby clams,
undrained
2 tablespoons chopped parsley
grated orange rind, to garnish

1 Melt the butter in a large pan and cook the bacon, onion, garlic and celery over low heat, stirring occasionally, for 5 minutes, or until soft but not brown. Add the potato, stock and thyme and bring to the boil.

2 Reduce the heat and simmer, covered, for 15 minutes. Stir in the tomato paste and tomato and return to the boil. Add the fish pieces, prawns and clams and simmer for 3 minutes.

3 Season to taste and stir in the parsley. Serve garnished with grated orange rind, if you want.

NUTRITION PER SERVE (6)
Protein 35 g; Fat 10 g; Carbohydrate 15 g;
Dietary Fibre 3 g; Cholesterol 200 mg;
1270 kJ (300 cal)

COOK'S FILE

Note: Prawns are not in a traditional chowder but are an excellent addition.

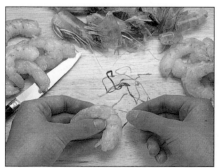

Devein the prawns by gently making a slit down the back and removing the vein.

Cook the bacon and vegetables over low heat until softened.

Add the potato, stock and chopped thyme and bring to the boil.

GAZPACHO

Preparation time: 40 minutes
 + 3 hours refrigeration
Total cooking time: Nil
Serves 4–6

750 g (1½ lb) ripe tomatoes
1 Lebanese cucumber, chopped
1 green capsicum, chopped
2–3 cloves garlic, crushed
1–2 tablespoons finely
   chopped black olives
   (optional)
⅓ cup (80 ml/2¾ fl oz) red or
   white wine vinegar

¼ cup (60 ml/2 fl oz) olive oil
1 tablespoon tomato paste

Accompaniments
1 onion, finely chopped
1 red capsicum, finely chopped
2 spring onions, finely chopped
1 Lebanese cucumber, finely
   chopped
2 hard-boiled eggs, chopped
chopped mint or parsley
Garlic and herb croutons
   (see page 99)

1 Score a cross in the base of each tomato. Cover with boiling water for 1 minute, plunge into cold water, drain and peel away the skins. Chop the flesh so finely that it is almost a purée.
2 Mix together the tomato, cucumber, capsicum, garlic, olives, vinegar, oil, and tomato paste, and season to taste. Cover and refrigerate for 2–3 hours.
3 Use 2–3 cups (750 ml/24 fl oz) of chilled water to thin the soup to your taste. Serve chilled, with the chopped onion, capsicum, spring onion, cucumber, boiled egg, herbs and croutons served separately for diners to add to their own bowls.

NUTRITION PER SERVE (6)
Protein 5 g; Fat 2 g; Carbohydrate 7 g;
Dietary Fibre 4 g; Cholesterol 70 mg;
310 kJ (75 cal)

Halve the cucumber lengthways, cut into strips and chop finely.

Put the tomatoes in a heatproof bowl and cover with boiling water.

Using a sharp knife, chop the tomato flesh very finely to a purée.

LENTIL AND SPINACH SOUP

Preparation time: 25 minutes
Total cooking time: 1 hour
Serves 8

½ cup (95 g/3 oz) brown lentils
2 tablespoons vegetable oil
1 leek, chopped
1 onion, chopped
1 stick celery, chopped

600 g (1¼ lb) potatoes, chopped
4 cups (1 litre) chicken stock
   (see page 82)
250 g (8 oz) English spinach

1 Put the lentils in a pan. Cover with water and bring to the boil, reduce the heat and simmer for 20 minutes, or until tender; drain.
2 Heat the oil in a large pan. Cook the leek, onion and celery for 5 minutes, or until softened. Add the potato and cook, stirring frequently, for

10 minutes. Add the stock and bring to the boil. Reduce the heat and simmer, covered, for 20 minutes, or until the potato is tender.
3 Remove the stalks from the spinach, wash the leaves well, add to the soup and cook for 1–2 minutes. Purée in a food processor, return to the pan, add the lentils and reheat.

NUTRITION PER SERVE
Protein 5 g; Fat 5 g; Carbohydrate 15 g;
Dietary Fibre 4 g; Cholesterol 0 mg;
505 kJ (120 cal)

Place the lentils in a pan and cover with plenty of cold water.

Cook the leek, onion and celery until soft, then add the chopped potato.

Add the cooked and drained lentils to the puréed soup in the pan.

Gazpacho (top)
with Lentil and spinach soup

SEAFOOD LAKSA

Preparation time: 45 minutes
Total cooking time: 40–45 minutes
Serves 4–6

1 kg (2 lb) raw prawns
1/2 cup (125 ml/4 fl oz) oil
2–6 red chillies, seeded
1 onion, roughly chopped
3 cloves garlic, peeled and
    halved
2 cm (3/4 inch) piece of ginger
    or galangal, quartered
1 teaspoon ground turmeric
1 tablespoon ground coriander
3 stalks lemon grass, white part
    only, chopped
1–2 teaspoons shrimp paste
2 1/2 cups (600 ml/20 fl oz)
    coconut cream
2 teaspoons grated palm sugar
4 kaffir lime leaves
200 g (6 1/2 oz) packet fish balls
190 g (6 1/2 oz) packet fried bean
    curd pieces
250 g (8 oz) thin fresh egg
    noodles
250 g (8 oz) bean sprouts
1/3 cup (20 g/1 oz) chopped mint,
    to serve
1/4 cup (7 g/1/4 oz) coriander
    leaves, to serve

1 Peel and devein the prawns, and set the shells, heads and tails aside. Set the prawns aside separately.
2 To make the prawn stock, heat 2 tablespoons of the oil in a large, heavy-based pan and add the prawn shells, heads and tails. Stir until the heads are bright orange, then add 4 cups (1 litre) of water. Bring to the boil, reduce the heat and simmer for 15 minutes. Strain the stock through a fine sieve, discarding the shells. Wipe the pan clean.
3 Put the chillies, onion, garlic, ginger (or galangal), turmeric, coriander, lemon grass and 1/4 cup (60 ml/2 fl oz) of the prawn stock in a food processor and process until finely chopped.
4 Heat the remaining oil in the clean pan and add the chilli mixture and shrimp paste. Stir over low heat for 3 minutes, or until fragrant. Pour in the remaining stock and simmer for 10 minutes. Then add the coconut cream, palm sugar, kaffir lime leaves and 2 teaspoons of salt. Simmer for a further 5 minutes.
5 Add the prawns and simmer for 2 minutes, until they are just pink. Remove and set aside. Add the fish balls and bean curd and simmer gently until just heated through.
6 Bring a pan of water to the boil and cook the noodles for 2 minutes, then drain and place in a bowl. Lay the bean sprouts and prawns on the noodles and pour the soup over the top. Sprinkle with the chopped mint and coriander leaves, to serve.

NUTRITION PER SERVE (6)
Protein 50 g; Fat 50 g; Carbohydrate 40 g; Dietary Fibre 8 g; Cholesterol 270 mg; 3340 kJ (800 cal)

COOK'S FILE

Hint: For a really fiery soup, garnish with extra sliced red chilli.
Note: Laksa originated in Singapore and can also be made using fresh or dried rice noodles. Shredded cucumber can be added with the bean sprouts.
Variation: Laksa can be made without the fish balls or bean curd. Instead, use a combination of seafood or replace the seafood with bite-sized pieces of chicken or pork.

Wearing rubber gloves, halve the chillies lengthways and remove the seeds.

Stir-fry the prawn shells, heads and tails until they turn bright orange.

Put the chillies, onion, garlic, lemon grass, spices and stock in a food processor.

Add the shrimp paste to the pan and stir in with a wooden spoon.

Add the coconut cream, palm sugar, salt and lime leaves and simmer.

Stir the fish balls into the simmering soup, then the bean curd.

PEA AND HAM SOUP

Preparation time: 20 minutes
Total cooking time: 2 hours 45 minutes
Serves 6–8

1 tablespoon oil
2 onions, diced
2 carrots, diced
2 sticks celery, diced
1 parsnip, diced
1½ cups (330 g/10½ oz) green
    split peas
1 teaspoon black peppercorns
2 teaspoons dried thyme
    leaves

1 ham hock (850 g/1 lb 12 oz),
    cut into smaller pieces
    (ask your butcher to do this)

1 Heat the oil in a large pan and add the onion, carrot, celery and parsnip. Cook over low heat for 10 minutes, or until the vegetables have softened and the onion is translucent.
2 Add the split peas, peppercorns, thyme, the pieces of ham hock and 8 cups (2 litres) of water. Slowly bring to the boil, reduce the heat to low and simmer, covered, for 2½ hours, or until most of the meat has fallen off the bones and the vegetables and split peas are very soft. Stir occasionally.

3 Remove the bones from the pan, pulling off any of the meat that hasn't fallen away. Chop any large pieces and return to the pan. Season well with salt and pepper, if necessary.

NUTRITION PER SERVE (8)
Protein 20 g; Fat 10 g; Carbohydrate 7 g; Dietary Fibre 3 g; Cholesterol 55 mg; 845 kJ (200 cal)

COOK'S FILE

Serving suggestion: This soup goes very well with the Caramelised onion braids on page 107.
Note: Ham hocks can be quite salty, so check the amount of salt on the ham; if it is crusted it is too mature.

Using a sharp knife, dice the onions, carrots, celery and parsnip.

Add the pieces of ham hock to the softened vegetables in the pan.

Using a sharp knife, trim off any meat that hasn't fallen away from the bones.

RICH OXTAIL SOUP

Preparation time: 35 minutes
+ 2 hours refrigeration
Total cooking time: 2 hours 25 minutes
Serves 4

2 oxtails, cut into pieces
(ask your butcher to do this)
2 tablespoons olive oil
3 onions, chopped
4 cloves garlic, finely chopped
1 tablespoon plain flour
4 cups (1 litre) beef stock
(see page 82)
2 bay leaves, torn in half
2 tablespoons tomato paste

2 teaspoons Worcestershire
sauce
4 potatoes, chopped
2 parsnips, chopped
2 carrots, chopped
3 tomatoes, chopped
2 tablespoons chopped parsley

1 Cut the excess fat from the oxtail.
Heat the oil in a heavy-based pan over
medium heat. Add the oxtail, onion
and garlic and cook for 8 minutes,
turning regularly, or until well
browned. Add the flour and cook for
1 minute, stirring. Mix in 2 cups
(500 ml/16 fl oz) of the stock and bring
to the boil, stirring continuously.
Remove from the heat and refrigerate

for 2 hours, or until the fat can be
spooned off the surface.
2 Add the remaining stock, 4 cups
(1 litre) of water, the bay leaves,
1/2 teaspoon each of salt and pepper,
tomato paste and Worcestershire
sauce. Bring to the boil, reduce the
heat to low and simmer, covered, for
2 hours, stirring occasionally.
3 Add the potato, parsnip and carrot
and simmer for 10 minutes, or until
tender. Remove the bay leaves and
discard. Serve with the chopped
tomato and parsley.

NUTRITION PER SERVE
Protein 8 g; Fat 16 g; Carbohydrate 40 g;
Dietary Fibre 10 g; Cholesterol 10 mg;
1620 kJ (390 cal)

*Using a sharp knife, trim away the
excess fat from the oxtail.*

*Sprinkle the flour over the browned oxtail
and cook, stirring, for 1 minute.*

*Add the parsnip, carrot and potato
and simmer for 10 minutes.*

SMOKED HADDOCK CHOWDER

Preparation time: 20 minutes
Total cooking time: 35 minutes
Serves 4–6

500 g (1 lb) smoked haddock
1 potato, diced
1 stick celery, diced
1 onion, finely chopped
50 g (1¾ oz) butter
1 rasher bacon, rind removed
   and finely chopped
2 tablespoons plain flour
½ teaspoon dried mustard
½ teaspoon Worcestershire
   sauce
1 cup (250 ml/8 fl oz) milk
½ cup (15 g/½ oz) chopped
   parsley
¼ cup (60 ml/2 fl oz) cream
   (optional)

1 To make the fish stock, put the fish in a frying pan, cover with water and bring to the boil. Reduce the heat and simmer for 8 minutes, or until the fish flakes easily. Drain, reserving the fish stock, then peel, bone and flake the fish. Set aside.

2 Put the potato, celery and onion in a medium pan and pour over enough reserved fish stock to cover the vegetables. Bring to the boil, reduce the heat and simmer for 8 minutes, or until the vegetables are tender. Set aside.

3 Melt the butter in a large pan, add the bacon and cook, stirring, for 3 minutes. Add the flour, mustard and Worcestershire sauce and stir until combined. Cook for 1 minute. Remove from the heat and gradually pour in the milk, stirring continuously, until smooth. Return to the heat and stir for 5 minutes, until the mixture comes to the boil and has thickened. Stir in the vegetables and remaining stock, then add the parsley and fish. Simmer over low heat for 5 minutes, or until heated through. Taste for seasoning and serve with some cream, if you want.

NUTRITION PER SERVE (6)
Protein 20 g; Fat 10 g; Carbohydrate 8 g; Dietary Fibre 1 g; Cholesterol 90 mg; 970 kJ (230 cal)

COOK'S FILE

Note: Chowder is a thick, hearty soup, made with seafood, fish, vegetables or chicken.

Simmer the haddock in a frying pan until it flakes easily when lifted with a fork.

Lay the fish on paper towels to drain well, then flake into small pieces.

Gradually add the milk, stirring continuously with a wooden spoon.

ROAST PUMPKIN SOUP

Preparation time: 10 minutes
Total cooking time: 1 hour 45 minutes
Serves 6

2 tablespoons olive oil
1 clove garlic, crushed
1 1/2 teaspoons dried oregano
250 g (8 oz) Roma tomatoes,
    halved lengthways
850 g (1 lb 12 oz) butternut
    pumpkin, unpeeled, chopped
250 g (8 oz) carrots, quartered
180 g (6 oz) onions, quartered

200 g (6 1/2 oz) sweet potato,
    chopped
1 tablespoon chopped oregano
6 cups (1.5 litres) chicken stock
    (see page 82)
flaked toasted almonds and
    oregano sprigs, to garnish

1 Preheat the oven to moderately hot 190°C (375°F/Gas 5). Mix the oil, garlic, oregano and 1/2 teaspoon of salt. Put the tomatoes, cut-side-up, in a roasting tin with the pumpkin, carrot, onion and sweet potato. Brush with the oil mixture and bake for 1 1/2 hours. Cool. Scrape the flesh from the

pumpkin and put in a large pan with the vegetables, oregano and stock.
2 Bring to the boil, reduce the heat and simmer for 10 minutes. Cool and purée in a blender or food processor. Reheat and season to taste. Garnish with the almonds and oregano sprigs.

NUTRITION PER SERVE
Protein 6 g; Fat 10 g; Carbohydrate 20 g; Dietary Fibre 6 g; Cholesterol 0 mg; 880 kJ (210 cal)

COOK'S FILE

Serving suggestion: This soup goes very well with the Cheese and herb pull-apart loaf on page 106.

Brush the vegetables with the oil mixture, leaving the tomatoes cut-side-up.

Scrape the flesh from the pumpkin using a teaspoon.

Purée the soup in batches in a blender or food processor.

SCOTCH BROTH

Preparation time: 40 minutes
+ 1 hour soaking
+ overnight refrigeration
Total cooking time: 4 hours
Serves 8

1 kg (2 lb) lamb shanks, cut in
   half through the bone
   (ask your butcher to do this)
3 onions, chopped
3 turnips, chopped
2 carrots, chopped
1 tablespoon black peppercorns
1/2 cup (110 g/3 1/2 oz) pearl
   barley

1 carrot, diced, extra
2 onions, finely chopped, extra
1 leek, chopped
1 stick celery, diced
2 turnips, diced, extra
chopped flat-leaf parsley

1 To make the stock, put the lamb shanks, onion, turnip, carrot, peppercorns and 8 cups (2 litres) of water in a large pan. Bring to the boil, reduce the heat and simmer, covered, for 3 hours. Skim the surface as required.
2 Remove the shanks and any meat that has fallen off the bones and cool slightly. Remove the meat from the bones and finely chop, then cover and refrigerate. Strain the stock, discarding the vegetables. Cool the stock and refrigerate overnight, or until the fat has set on top and can be spooned off. Cover the barley with water and soak for 1 hour.
3 Put the stock in a large pan and gently reheat. Add the drained barley, extra carrot, onion, leek, celery and turnip. Bring to the boil, reduce the heat and simmer for 30 minutes, or until the barley and vegetables are just cooked. Return the meat to the pan and simmer for 5 minutes. Season well and serve with the parsley.

NUTRITION PER SERVE
Protein 35 g; Fat 3 g; Carbohydrate 20 g;
Dietary Fibre 6 g; Cholesterol 80 mg;
970 kJ (230 cal)

Use a skimmer or slotted spoon to skim the surface of the stock.

Place the barley in a bowl and cover with plenty of cold water.

The vegetables for the soup should be evenly and finely diced.

WATERCRESS AND POTATO SOUP

Preparation time: 30 minutes
Total cooking time: 50 minutes
Serves 6–8

30 g (1 oz) butter
2 onions, chopped
1–2 cloves garlic, chopped
1 kg (2 lb) potatoes, chopped
   into chunks
8 cups (2 litres) chicken stock
   (see page 82)
250 g (8 oz) watercress,
   trimmed
1/3 cup (80 ml/2³/4 fl oz) cream

Parmesan croutons
2 slices bread, crusts removed
1 tablespoon olive oil
1 tablespoon grated Parmesan

1 Heat the butter in a large pan. Cook the onion and garlic for 2–3 minutes, or until softened. Add the potato and stir for 1–2 minutes. Add the stock and bring to the boil. Reduce the heat and simmer for 30 minutes, or until the potato is cooked. Strain, reserving the cooking liquid.
2 Transfer the potato mixture to a food processor, pour on about half the cooking liquid and process until smooth. Return to the pan.
3 In a food processor, process the watercress and 2 cups (500 ml/16 fl oz) of the cooking liquid until smooth. Pour the watercress mixture, cream and any remaining cooking liquid into the pan and combine. Stir over low heat for 3 minutes, or until warmed through, but do not allow the soup to boil. Season to taste.
4 To make the croutons, preheat the oven to moderate 180°C (350°F/Gas 4). Cut the bread into cubes and mix with the oil and grated Parmesan. Bake for 10 minutes, or until golden. Serve the croutons on top of the soup.

NUTRITION PER SERVE (8)
Protein 6 g; Fat 10 g; Carbohydrate 20 g; Dietary Fibre 4 g; Cholesterol 25 mg; 880 kJ (210 cal)

Pour in half the cooking liquid over the potato mixture.

Quickly mix the bread cubes in the oil and Parmesan until well coated.

Process the watercress and liquid until smooth and pour into the pan.

MISO SOUP

Preparation time: 5–10 minutes
Total cooking time: 5 minutes
Serves 4

2 teaspoons dashi granules or
    powder (see Note)
3 tablespoons miso paste
    (see Note)
250 g (8 oz) silken tofu
2 spring onions

1 Mix the dashi granules or powder with 4 cups (1 litre) of cold water in a pan and bring to the boil. Reduce the heat and whisk in the miso paste.
2 Cut the tofu into small cubes and add to the soup. Slice the spring onions diagonally, separate the layers and add to the soup. Simmer gently for 2–3 minutes before serving.

NUTRITION PER SERVE
Protein 5 g; Fat 3 g; Carbohydrate 5 g;
Dietary Fibre 0 g; Cholesterol 0 mg;
255 kJ (60 cal)

COOK'S FILE

Note: Dashi is a basic stock used in Japanese cooking which is made by boiling dried kelp (seaweed) and dried bonito (fish). Instant dashi granules are sold in conveniently-sized jars or packets and vary in strength. Add more dashi to your soup if you want a stronger stock.

You can use yellow, white or red miso paste for this soup. Yellow miso is sweet and creamy; red miso is strong and salty.

Put the cold water in a pan and add the dashi granules or powder.

Add the miso paste to the pan and whisk until dissolved.

Slice the spring onions diagonally and separate the layers.

TOM KHA GAI

Preparation time: 20 minutes
Total cooking time: 20 minutes
Serves 4

5 cm (2 inch) piece of fresh
    galangal or 5 slices of dried
    galangal (see Note)
6 kaffir lime leaves
1 stem lemon grass, white part
    only, quartered
2 cups (500 ml/16 fl oz) coconut
    milk
2 cups (500 ml/16 fl oz) chicken
    stock (see page 82)

3 chicken breast fillets, cut into
    thin strips
1–2 teaspoons finely chopped
    red chillies
¼ cup (60 ml/2 fl oz) lime juice
2 tablespoons fish sauce
1 teaspoon soft brown sugar
¼ cup (15 g/½ oz) coriander
    leaves

1 Peel the galangal and cut into thin slices. Mix the galangal, kaffir lime leaves and lemon grass with the coconut milk and stock in a medium pan. Bring to the boil, reduce the heat to low and simmer for 10 minutes, stirring occasionally.

2 Add the chicken strips and chilli and simmer for 8 minutes. Mix in the lime juice, fish sauce and sugar. Serve with the coriander leaves and garnish with coriander sprigs, if you want.

NUTRITION PER SERVE
Protein 40 g; Fat 30 g; Carbohydrate 5 g;
Dietary Fibre 0 g; Cholesterol 80 mg;
1840 kJ (440 cal)

COOK'S FILE

Note: If you can't find fresh galangal, use 5 large slices of dried galangal instead. Soak in 1 cup (250 ml/8 fl oz) of boiling water for 10 minutes, drain then cut into thin slices.

Using a sharp knife, cut the chicken breast fillets into thin strips.

Using a vegetable peeler, peel the fresh galangal and slice thinly.

Add the soft brown sugar to the soup and stir to dissolve.

Miso soup (top)
with Tom kha gai

SAFFRON FISH SOUP

Preparation time: 20 minutes
Total cooking time: 30 minutes
Serves 4

1 kg (2 lb) white fish bones
    (heads and trimmings),
    chopped
2 cups (500 ml/16 fl oz) dry
    white wine
1 onion, chopped
1 carrot, chopped
1 stick celery, chopped
1 bay leaf
6 black peppercorns
3/4 teaspoon saffron threads
50 g (13/4 oz) butter
1/4 cup (30 g/1 oz) plain flour
12 scallops, trimmed
250 g (8 oz) boneless white fish
    fillets, cut into cubes
1 cup (250 ml/8 fl oz) cream

1 To make the saffron fish stock, place the fish bones, 3 cups (750 ml/ 24 fl oz) of water, the wine, onion, carrot, celery, bay leaf and peppercorns in a large pan. Bring to the boil slowly, skimming the surface as required. Simmer, covered, for 20 minutes. Strain and discard the fish and vegetables. Take 4 cups (1 litre) of the hot stock and stir in the saffron threads. (If you have any stock leftover, freeze it for use in another recipe.)

2 Melt the butter in a large pan and stir in the flour. Cook, stirring continuously, over low heat for 3 minutes but do not allow the mixture to colour. Remove from the heat and gradually pour in the reserved fish stock. Return to the heat and stir continuously until the mixture boils and thickens slightly. Add the scallops and fish cubes, bring back to the boil and simmer for 1–2 minutes.

3 Stir in the cream and reheat gently, but do not allow the soup to boil. Season to taste with salt and freshly ground white pepper. Garnish with sprigs of chervil, if you want.

NUTRITION PER SERVE
Protein 25 g; Fat 40 g; Carbohydrate 10 g; Dietary Fibre 1 g; Cholesterol 190 mg; 2425 kJ (580 cal)

Using a sharp knife, remove the dark vein from the scallops.

Add the bay leaf and peppercorns to the pan.

Combine the reserved hot fish stock and saffron threads in a jug or bowl.

Add the scallops and fish cubes to the soup and simmer for 1–2 minutes.

COCK-A-LEEKIE

Preparation time: 10 minutes
+ 2 hours refrigeration
Total cooking time: 1 hour 40 minutes
Serves 4–6

1.5 kg (3 lb) chicken
250 g (8 oz) chicken giblets
  (optional), (see Note)
1 onion, sliced
8 cups (2 litres) chicken stock
  (see page 82)
4 leeks, thinly sliced
1/4 teaspoon ground coriander
pinch of nutmeg

1 bouquet garni
12 pitted prunes
pinch of cayenne pepper
3 sprigs thyme
thyme sprigs, extra, to serve

1 To make the chicken stock, put the chicken in a large pan and add the giblets (if using), onion and stock. Bring to the boil, skimming the surface as required. Add the leek, coriander, nutmeg and bouquet garni. Reduce the heat, cover and simmer for 1 1/4 hours.

2 Remove the chicken and bouquet garni and lift out the giblets with a slotted spoon. Cool the stock, then refrigerate for 2 hours. Spoon off the fat from the surface and discard. Remove the meat from the bones and shred. Discard the skin and carcass.

3 Return the meat to the soup with the prunes, cayenne pepper and thyme. Simmer for 20 minutes. Season to taste and garnish with the extra thyme sprigs, if you want.

NUTRITION PER SERVE (6)
Protein 60 g; Fat 6 g; Carbohydrate 7 g;
Dietary Fibre 1 g; Cholesterol 125 mg;
1310 kJ (315 cal)

COOK'S FILE

Note: The chicken giblets are optional but will give great flavour.

Trim the ends from the leeks and slice thinly, including some green parts.

Add the chicken stock to the pan with the chicken, giblets (if using) and onion.

Add the prunes and thyme sprigs to the soup and stir to combine.

ROASTED TOMATO SOUP

Preparation time: 20 minutes
Total cooking time: 1 hour 10 minutes
Serves 4

1 kg (2 lb) Roma tomatoes
5 cloves garlic, unpeeled
5 tablespoons olive oil
1 teaspoon dried basil
3 tablespoons olive oil, extra
1 onion, finely chopped
1 red chilli, finely chopped
2 tablespoons balsamic vinegar
2 teaspoons soft brown sugar
1 tablespoon plain flour

4 cups (1 litre) vegetable stock
(see page 83)
1/4 cup (7 g/1/4 oz) chopped flat-
leaf parsley, to serve

1 Preheat the oven to moderately hot 200°C (400°F/Gas 6). Halve the tomatoes and lay cut-side-up in a baking tray with the garlic. Add the oil, some seasoning and the basil. Roast for 30 minutes. Take the garlic out after 20 minutes if it is drying out.
2 Heat the extra oil in a heavy-based pan. Add the onion and chilli and cook, covered, for 10 minutes over medium heat, stirring frequently.
3 Chop the tomatoes and squeeze the

garlic pulp from their skins. Add to the pan along with the vinegar and sugar. Cook, stirring, for 1 minute. Stir in the flour and cook for 30 seconds.
4 Remove from the heat and add the stock. Return to the heat and bring to the boil, stirring occasionally. Simmer for 5 minutes. Season to taste and add the parsley.

NUTRITION PER SERVE
Protein 4 g; Fat 40 g; Carbohydrate 10 g; Dietary Fibre 5 g; Cholesterol 0 mg; 1670 kJ (400 cal)

COOK'S FILE

Serving suggestion: Serve with the Rosemary bread trios on page 85.

Sprinkle the dried basil over the halved tomatoes and unpeeled garlic cloves.

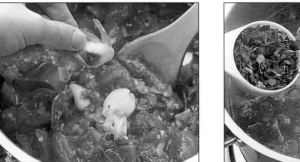

Squeeze the garlic pulp from their skins and add to the pan.

Add the chopped flat-leaf parsley to the soup just before serving.

Halve the tomatoes and scoop out the seeds with a teaspoon.

Brown the shanks in 2 batches, remove with tongs and drain on paper towels.

RUSTIC HOT POT

Preparation time: 40 minutes
  + 1 hour refrigeration
Total cooking time: 2 hours
Serves 4

2 tablespoons olive oil
8 lamb shanks
2 onions, sliced
4 cloves garlic, finely chopped
3 bay leaves, torn in half
1–2 teaspoons hot paprika
2 teaspoons sweet paprika
1 tablespoon plain flour
3 tablespoons tomato paste
6 cups (1.5 litres) vegetable
  stock (see page 83)
4 potatoes, chopped
4 carrots, sliced
3 sticks celery, thickly sliced
3 tomatoes, seeded and chopped

1 To make the lamb stock, heat 1 tablespoon of the oil in a large, heavy-based pan over medium heat. Brown the shanks well in two batches and drain on paper towels.

2 Add the remaining tablespoon of oil to the pan and cook the onion, garlic and bay leaves over low heat for 10 minutes, stirring regularly. Add the paprikas and flour and cook, stirring continuously, for 2 minutes. Gradually add the combined tomato paste and stock. Bring to the boil, stirring continuously, and return the shanks to the pan. Reduce the heat to low and simmer, covered, for 1½ hours, stirring occasionally.

3 Remove the bay leaves and discard. Remove the shanks, allow to cool slightly and then cut the meat from the bone. Discard the bones. Cut the meat into pieces and refrigerate. Refrigerate the stock for about 1 hour, or until fat forms on the surface and can be spooned off.

4 Return the meat to the soup along with the potato, carrot and celery and bring to the boil. Reduce the heat and simmer for 15 minutes. Season and add the chopped tomato to serve.

Stir the paprikas and flour into the onion mixture until it just begins to colour.

Spoon off the fat that forms on the surface of the soup.

NUTRITION PER SERVE
Protein 70 g; Fat 15 g; Carbohydrate 30 g; Dietary Fibre 8 g; Cholesterol 170 mg; 2200 kJ (525 cal)

BEEF CONSOMME

Preparation time: 30 minutes
+ overnight refrigeration
Total cooking time: 5 hours
Serves 4–6

1 kg (2 lb) gravy beef, cut into
    small pieces
500 g (1 lb) beef bones
    including marrow, cut into
    small pieces (ask your
    butcher to do this)
1 leek, cut into small pieces
2 onions, quartered
2 carrots, chopped
2 sticks celery, chopped
6 black peppercorns
6 whole cloves
3 sprigs thyme
3 sprigs parsley
3 bay leaves
1 egg shell, crumbled
1 egg white, lightly beaten
2 tablespoons chopped parsley

1 Preheat the oven to moderate 180°C
(350°F/Gas 4). Place the gravy beef
and beef bones in a single layer in a
baking dish. Bake for 45 minutes, or
until lightly browned, turning once.
2 Put the meat, bones, vegetables,
peppercorns, cloves, herbs, bay leaves
and 1 teaspoon of salt in a large pan.
Add 3 litres of water and slowly bring
to the boil. Reduce the heat to low,
cover and simmer for 4 hours. Set
aside to cool slightly. Remove the
larger pieces of meat and discard.
Ladle the liquid through a muslin-
lined sieve into a bowl. Discard the
remaining meat and vegetables.
3 Cover the liquid and refrigerate for
several hours, or overnight. Spoon off
the fat from the surface. Return to a
clean pan with the egg shell and the
lightly beaten egg white.
4 Slowly heat the stock to simmering
and simmer for 10 minutes. A frothy
scum will form on the surface.
Remove from the heat and leave for
10 minutes. Skim the surface and ladle
the stock through a muslin-lined sieve.
Reheat, season if needed, and serve
with the chopped parsley.

NUTRITION PER SERVE (6)
Protein 35 g; Fat 5 g; Carbohydrate 4 g;
Dietary Fibre 2 g; Cholesterol 110 mg;
858 kJ (205 cal)

*Lay the gravy beef and bones in a single
layer in a large baking dish.*

*Carefully ladle the stock into the muslin-
lined sieve placed over a bowl.*

*Gently stir in the egg shell and egg white
with a balloon whisk or wooden spoon.*

*A froth will form on the surface as the
stock gently simmers.*

SPRING VEGETABLE SOUP

Preparation time: 30 minutes
  + overnight soaking
Total cooking time: 1 hour 15 minutes
Serves 8

1/2 cup (105 g/3 1/2 oz) pinto
  beans
2 teaspoons olive oil
2 onions, finely chopped
2 cloves garlic, finely chopped
10 cups (2.5 litres) vegetable
  stock (see page 83)
2 sticks celery, finely chopped
2 carrots
2 potatoes
150 g (5 oz) green beans
2 zucchini
100 g (3 1/2 oz) shelled peas
  (see Hint)
2 tablespoons chopped flat-leaf
  parsley

1 Soak the pinto beans in plenty of cold water overnight. Drain.
2 Heat the oil in a large pan, add the onion and cook over low heat until soft and translucent. Add the garlic and cook for 1 minute further. Add the pinto beans, stock and celery and bring to the boil. Reduce the heat to low and simmer, covered, for 45 minutes, or until the beans are almost cooked.
3 Finely chop the carrots, potatoes, green beans and zucchini and add to the pan. Simmer gently for 15 minutes, or until the vegetables are almost cooked. Stir in the peas and simmer for a further 10 minutes.
4 Season well and stir through the chopped parsley.

NUTRITION PER SERVE
Protein 5 g; Fat 2 g; Carbohydrate 10 g;
Dietary Fibre 5 g; Cholesterol 0 mg;
235 kJ (60 cal)

COOK'S FILE

Note: If pinto beans are hard to find, you can easily substitute them with borlotti beans or the smaller haricot beans.
Hint: If you can't find fresh peas, use frozen peas. Thaw and add during the last 5 minutes of cooking.
Serving suggestion: Serve with the Sunflower bread on page 102.

Add the drained pinto beans to the pan and stir in with a wooden spoon.

Chop all the vegetables into small, even-sized dice.

CHICKEN AND VEGETABLE SOUP

Preparation time: 1 hour + refrigeration
Total cooking time: 1 hour 25 minutes
Serves 6–8

1.5 kg (2½ lb) chicken
2 carrots, roughly chopped
2 sticks celery, roughly chopped
1 onion, quartered
4 parsley sprigs
2 bay leaves
4 black peppercorns
50 g (1¾ oz) butter
2 tablespoons plain flour
2 potatoes, chopped
250 g (8 oz) butternut pumpkin,
    chopped into bite-sized pieces
2 carrots, extra, cut into
    matchsticks
1 leek, cut into matchsticks
3 sticks celery, extra, cut into
    matchsticks
100 g (3½ oz) green beans, cut
    into short lengths or baby
    green beans, halved
200 g (6½ oz) broccoli, cut into
    small florets
100 g (3½ oz) sugar snap peas,
    trimmed
50 g (1¾ oz) English spinach
    leaves, shredded
½ cup (125 ml/4 fl oz) cream
¼ cup (15 g/½ oz) chopped
    parsley

1 To make the chicken stock, place the chicken in a large pan with the carrot, celery, onion, parsley, bay leaves, 2 teaspoons of salt and the peppercorns. Add 3 litres of water. Bring to the boil, reduce the heat and simmer for 1 hour, skimming the surface as required. Allow to cool for at least 30 minutes. Strain and reserve the liquid.

2 Remove the chicken and allow to cool enough to handle. Discard the skin, then cut or pull the flesh from the bones and shred into small pieces. Set the chicken meat aside.

3 Heat the butter in a large pan over medium heat and, when foaming, add the flour. Cook, stirring, for 1 minute. Remove from the heat and gradually stir in the stock. Return to the heat and bring to the boil, stirring continuously. Add the potato, pumpkin and extra carrot and simmer for 7 minutes. Add the leek, extra celery and beans and simmer for a further 5 minutes. Finally, add the broccoli and sugar snap peas and cook for a further 3 minutes.

4 Just before serving, add the chicken meat, spinach, cream and chopped parsley. Reheat gently but do not allow the soup to boil. Keep stirring until the spinach has wilted. Season to taste with plenty of salt and freshly ground black pepper. Serve immediately.

NUTRITION PER SERVE (8)
Protein 50 g; Fat 15 g; Carbohydrate 15 g; Dietary Fibre 6 g; Cholesterol 130 mg; 1700 kJ (400 cal)

COOK'S FILE

Hint: Do not overcook the vegetables, they should be tender yet crispy.
Note: The chicken stock (up to the end of Step 1) can be made 1 day ahead and kept, covered, in the refrigerator. This can, in fact, be beneficial—before reheating the stock, spoon off the fat which will have formed on the surface.
Serving suggestion: This soup goes very well with the Fougasse on page 88.

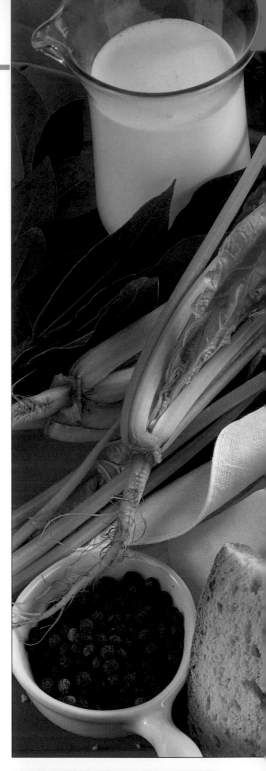

Cut the extra celery into short lengths, then into matchsticks.

Using a knife, trim the tops from the peas, pulling down to remove the string.

Add the parsley sprigs and bay leaves to the pan.

Remove the skin from the chicken, then shred the meat.

Add the potato, pumpkin and extra carrot to the boiling soup.

Pour in the cream and stir until the spinach has wilted. Reheat gently.

ROASTED LEEK, GARLIC AND BACON SOUP

Preparation time: 25 minutes
Total cooking time: 1 hour 30 minutes
Serves 4–6

1 tablespoon olive oil
20 g (³/4 oz) butter
2 rashers bacon, chopped
3 leeks, chopped
2 cloves garlic, chopped
1 stick celery, coarsely chopped
2 zucchini, coarsely chopped
2 bay leaves
6 cups (1.5 litres) chicken stock
    (see page 82)
¹/3 cup (80 ml/2³/4 fl oz) cream

¹/4 cup (15 g/¹/2 oz) finely
    chopped parsley
2 rashers bacon, extra, to serve

1 Preheat the oven to warm 160°C (315°F/Gas 2–3). Heat the oil and butter in a large roasting tin. Add the bacon rashers and stir over medium heat for 1–2 minutes. Add the leek, garlic, celery, zucchini and bay leaves and cook, stirring, for 2–3 minutes, without allowing to brown.
2 Transfer the roasting tin to the oven and roast the vegetables and bacon for 40 minutes, turning a couple of times. Cover with foil if starting to brown. Transfer to a large pan, pour on the stock and bring to the boil. Lower the heat and simmer for

30 minutes. Cool slightly, strain and return the liquid to the pan. Remove the bay leaves.
3 Put the vegetables and bacon in a food processor with a ladleful of the cooking liquid and process until smooth, adding more liquid if necessary. Return the purée to the pan with the liquid and add some pepper, the cream and parsley. Reheat gently.
4 To make the bacon garnish, trim off the rind and excess fat from the bacon and grill until crisp. Drain on paper towels, then crumble with your fingers and serve on top of the soup.

NUTRITION PER SERVE (6)
Protein 7 g; Fat 15 g; Carbohydrate 2 g; Dietary Fibre 1 g; Cholesterol 45 mg; 640 kJ (150 cal)

Turn the vegetables during cooking and cover with foil to prevent browning.

Process the vegetables and bacon until smooth. Add more liquid if necessary.

Grill the bacon until it is very crisp, then crumble to make a garnish.

PORK BALL AND VEGETABLE SOUP

Preparation time: 45 minutes
Total cooking time: 10 minutes
Serves 6–8

90 g (3 oz) stale white bread,
  crusts removed
500 g (1 lb) pork mince
2 teaspoons chopped coriander
  roots and stems
3 teaspoons chopped coriander
  leaves
1/2 teaspoon five-spice powder
1 teaspoon grated ginger
1 egg white
3 cups (270 g/9 oz) bean sprouts

2 teaspoons sesame oil
9 cups (2.25 litres) chicken
  stock (see page 82)
1 small red chilli, chopped
2 carrots, cut into strips
2 sticks celery, cut into strips
6 spring onions, cut into strips
1 1/2 tablespoons lime juice
coriander leaves, to serve

1 Line a baking tin with baking paper. Cover the bread with cold water, then squeeze out the liquid. Mix with the mince, coriander, five-spice powder, ginger, egg white and 1/4 teaspoon each of salt and pepper.
2 Roll 1/2 tablespoons of the mixture into balls and lay in the tin. Divide the bean sprouts among bowls. Mix the sesame oil and stock in a large pan, bring to the boil and add the balls in batches. Return to the boil and, when they float, divide among the bowls.
3 Add the chilli, carrot, celery and spring onion to the stock, bring to the boil and simmer for 1 minute. Remove from the heat, season to taste and add the lime juice. Ladle into bowls and top with a few coriander leaves.

NUTRITION PER SERVE (8)
Protein 4 g; Fat 8 g; Carbohydrate 10 g; Dietary Fibre 2 g; Cholesterol 2 mg; 575 kJ (160 cal)

COOK'S FILE

Note: Five-spice is a mixture of Szechwan pepper, star anise, fennel, cloves and cinnamon.

Coarsely chop the roots and stems from the coriander and then chop finely.

Cut the vegetables into short lengths, then cut into fine (julienne) strips.

Soak the bread in water, then squeeze out the liquid.

MEXICAN BEAN CHOWDER

Preparation time: 20 minutes
 + overnight soaking
Total cooking time: 1 hour 10 minutes
Serves 6

3/4 cup (155 g/5 oz) dried red
    kidney beans
3/4 cup (165 g/5¹/2 oz) dried
    Mexican black beans
1 tablespoon oil
1 onion, chopped
2 cloves garlic, crushed
¹/2-1 teaspoon chilli powder
1 tablespoon ground cumin
2 teaspoons ground coriander
2 x 400 g (13 oz) cans chopped
    tomatoes
3 cups (750 ml/24 fl oz)
    vegetable stock (see page 83)
1 red capsicum, chopped
1 green capsicum, chopped
440 g (14 oz) can corn kernels
2 tablespoons tomato paste
grated Cheddar, to serve
sour cream, to serve

1 Soak the kidney beans and black beans in separate bowls in plenty of cold water overnight. Drain. Place in a large pan, cover with water and bring to the boil. Reduce the heat and simmer for 45 minutes, or until tender. Drain.

2 Heat the oil in a large pan, add the onion and cook over medium heat until soft. Add the garlic, chilli powder, cumin and coriander and cook for 1 minute. Stir in the tomato, stock, capsicum, corn and tomato paste. Cook, covered, for 25–30 minutes. Add the beans during the last 10 minutes of cooking. Stir occasionally.

3 Serve topped with the grated Cheddar and a spoonful of sour cream.

NUTRITION PER SERVE
Protein 20 g; Fat 7 g; Carbohydrate 40 g;
Dietary Fibre 20 g; Cholesterol 3 mg;
1250 kJ (300 cal)

COOK'S FILE

Serving suggestion: This soup goes very well with the Sour cream polenta bread on page 109.
Note: Mexican black beans are also known as black turtle beans.

Soak the red kidney beans and black beans in separate bowls overnight.

Add the tomato, stock, capsicum, corn and tomato paste.

TOM YAM GOONG

Preparation time: 25 minutes
Total cooking time: 45 minutes
Serves 4–6

500 g (1 lb) raw prawns
1 tablespoon oil
2 tablespoons Thai red curry
   paste
2 tablespoons tamarind purée
2 teaspoons turmeric
1 teaspoon chopped red chillies
4 kaffir lime leaves, shredded
2 tablespoons fish sauce
2 tablespoons lime juice

2 teaspoons soft brown sugar
coriander leaves, to serve

1 Peel and devein the prawns, leaving the tails intact. Heat the oil in a large pan and cook the prawn shells and heads for 10 minutes over medium high heat, tossing frequently, until the heads are deep orange.
2 Add 1 cup (250 ml/8 fl oz) water and the curry paste. Boil for 5 minutes, or until reduced slightly. Add another 8 cups (2 litres) of water and simmer for 20 minutes. Strain, discarding the shells and heads, and return the stock to the pan.
3 Add the tamarind, turmeric, chilli

and kaffir lime leaves; bring to the boil and cook for 2 minutes. Add the prawns and cook for 5 minutes, or until pink. Mix in the fish sauce, lime juice and sugar. Serve sprinkled with coriander leaves.

NUTRITION PER SERVE (6)
Protein 17 g; Fat 6 g; Carbohydrate 2 g; Dietary Fibre 0 g; Cholesterol 125 mg; 560 kJ (135 cal)

COOK'S FILE

Hint: If you can't find tamarind purée, soak one quarter of a block of tamarind in warm water for 10 minutes, work the mixture with your fingertips and remove the stones.

Add the red curry paste and a cup of water to the pan.

Add the tamarind, turmeric, chilli and kaffir lime leaves.

Add the prawns to the boiling soup mixture and cook until pink.

THAI-STYLE CHICKEN AND BABY CORN SOUP

Preparation time: 30 minutes
Total cooking time: 15 minutes
Serves 4

150 g (5 oz) whole baby corn
1 tablespoon oil
2 stalks lemon grass, white part only, very finely sliced
2 tablespoons finely grated ginger
6 spring onions, chopped
1 red chilli, finely chopped
4 cups (1 litre) chicken stock (see page 82)

1½ cups (375 ml/12 fl oz) coconut milk
250 g (8 oz) chicken breast fillets, thinly sliced
130 g (4¼ oz) creamed corn
1 tablespoon soy sauce
2 tablespoons finely chopped chives, to serve
1 red chilli, thinly sliced, to serve

1 Cut the baby corn in half or quarters lengthways, depending on their size. Set aside.
2 Heat the oil in a pan over medium heat and cook the lemon grass, ginger, spring onion and chilli for 1 minute, stirring continuously. Add the stock and coconut milk and bring to the boil—do not cover or the coconut milk will curdle.
3 Stir in the corn, chicken and creamed corn and simmer for 8 minutes, or until the corn and chicken are just tender. Add the soy sauce, season well and serve garnished with the chives and chilli.

NUTRITION PER SERVE
Protein 20 g; Fat 25 g; Carbohydrate 15 g; Dietary Fibre 3 g; Cholesterol 30 mg; 1520 kJ (360 cal)

COOK'S FILE

Note: Canned baby corn can be substituted for fresh corn. Add during the last 2 minutes of cooking.

Grate the peeled ginger on the fine side of the grater.

Cut the baby corn lengthways into halves or quarters.

Add the corn, chicken and creamed corn to the pan.

PARSNIP AND MUSTARD SOUP

Preparation time: 25 minutes
Total cooking time: 30 minutes
Serves 4–6

30 g (1 oz) butter
1 onion, chopped
750 g (1½ lb) parsnips, chopped
4 cups (1 litre) chicken stock
    (see page 82)
½ cup (125 ml/4 fl oz) milk
½ cup (125 ml/4 fl oz) cream
2–3 tablespoons wholegrain
    mustard
2 tablespoons chopped flat-leaf
    parsley, to serve

1 Melt the butter in a large pan, add the onion and cook over moderate heat, stirring occasionally, until soft but not brown.
2 Add the parsnip and stock and bring to the boil. Simmer, covered, for 25 minutes, or until the parsnip is tender. Set aside to cool slightly.
3 Blend the soup in batches, in a blender or food processor. Return to the pan, add the milk and cream and reheat gently, but do not allow the soup to boil. Stir in the wholegrain mustard and season to taste with salt and freshly ground black pepper. Serve topped with the chopped parsley.

NUTRITION PER SERVE (6)
Protein 4 g; Fat 15 g; Carbohydrate 15 g;
Dietary Fibre 4 g; Cholesterol 45 mg;
850 kJ (200 cal)

COOK'S FILE

Serving suggestion: This soup goes very well with the Pumpkin damper on page 91.

Cut the peeled parsnips into strips, then chop into small pieces.

Add the parsnip and chicken stock to the pan.

Using a wooden spoon, stir in the wholegrain mustard.

SPICY TOMATO AND CHICKPEA SOUP

Preparation time: 20 minutes
  + overnight soaking
Total cooking time: 1 hour 25 minutes
Serves 4

1 cup (220 g/7 oz) dried
  chickpeas
1 tablespoon oil
1 onion, finely chopped
2 cloves garlic, crushed
1/2–1 teaspoon chopped chilli
425 g (14 oz) can chopped
  tomatoes
2 cups (500 ml/8 fl oz)
  vegetable stock (see page 83)
2 teaspoons balsamic vinegar

1 Soak the chickpeas overnight in cold water. Drain. Cook the chickpeas in a large pan of boiling water for 1 hour, or until tender. Drain well.

2 Heat the oil in a large pan, add the onion and cook for 5 minutes, or until very soft and lightly golden. Add the garlic and chilli and cook for 1 minute, then add the tomato and stock.

3 Take 1 cup (250 ml/8 fl oz) of the soup mixture and transfer the rest to a food processor. Process until smooth, and return to the pan with the reserved soup mixture and chickpeas. Bring to the boil and simmer for 15 minutes. Stir in the vinegar and season to taste.

NUTRITION PER SERVE
Protein 10 g; Fat 8 g; Carbohydrate 25 g; Dietary Fibre 8 g; Cholesterol 0 mg; 895 kJ (215 cal)

COOK'S FILE

Serving suggestion: Serve with the Olive spirals on page 108.

Cook the chickpeas in plenty of boiling water for 1 hour, or until tender.

Add the chopped garlic and chilli (to your taste) to the onion in the pan.

Pour the reserved soup mixture back into the pan.

VICHYSSOISE

Preparation time: 10 minutes
Total cooking time: 45 minutes
Serves 4–6

80 g (2¾ oz) butter
4 leeks, white part only, thinly
   sliced
1 white onion, thinly sliced
500 g (1 lb) potatoes, chopped
¼ teaspoon ground coriander
pinch of ground nutmeg
1 bay leaf
1 stick celery, quartered

3½ cups (875 ml/28 fl oz)
   chicken or vegetable stock
   (see page 82)
2 teaspoons lemon juice
½ cup (125 ml/4 fl oz) cream
chives, snipped, to garnish

1 Melt the butter in a large pan, add the leek and onion and fry gently, stirring occasionally, for 8–10 minutes, or until the vegetables are soft but not brown.
2 Add the potato, coriander, nutmeg, bay leaf, celery, stock and lemon juice. Bring to the boil, cover and simmer for 30 minutes, or until the vegetables

are tender. Remove from the heat and allow to cool slightly. Remove the bay leaf and celery and discard.
3 Transfer to a food processor and process until smooth. Return to the pan. Whisk in the cream, then reheat gently without boiling. Serve either hot or cold, garnished with the chives.

NUTRITION PER SERVE (6)
Protein 9 g; Fat 20 g; Carbohydrate 20 g; Dietary Fibre 8 g; Cholesterol 90 mg; 1300 kJ (310 cal)

COOK'S FILE

Serving suggestion: Delicious garnished with crumbled fried bacon.

Add the chopped potato to the vegetables in the pan.

Allow the soup to cool a little before puréeing in batches until smooth.

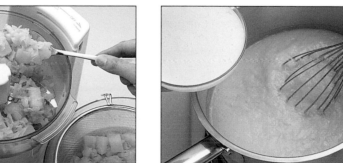

Whisk in the cream and then reheat the soup without boiling.

LOBSTER BISQUE

Preparation time: 60 minutes
Total cooking time: 1 hour
Serves 4

400 g (13 oz) raw lobster tail
100 g (3¹/₂ oz) butter, softened
7 spring onions, chopped
1 onion, chopped
1 carrot, chopped
4 cups (1 litre) fish stock
   (see page 83)
4 sprigs parsley
1 bay leaf
4 peppercorns
¹/₃ cup (40 g/1¹/₄ oz) plain flour
1³/₄ cups (440 ml/14 fl oz)
   tomato purée
1 tablespoon sherry, optional
¹/₂ cup (125 ml/4 fl oz) cream
pinch of nutmeg
2 teaspoons chopped tarragon

1 Cut the lobster tail in half lengthways.
2 Melt half the butter in a pan, add the spring onion and onion and cook for 5 minutes, or until soft but not coloured. Add the carrot and cook for 2 minutes. Add the lobster halves, fish stock, parsley, bay leaf, peppercorns and 2¹/₂ cups (600 ml/20 fl oz) of water. Bring to the boil, reduce the heat and simmer for 20 minutes, skimming the surface as required.
3 Remove the lobster from the stock, cool slightly and take the meat from the shells. Crush the shells and return to the pan. Continue simmering for a further 40 minutes. Strain the stock, then strain again through a sieve lined with 2 layers of damp muslin.
4 Cut some thin slices from the lobster to use as a garnish and set

aside. In a blender, blend the remaining lobster flesh with a little of the strained stock until smooth. Mix the flour and remaining butter to a paste. Add the puréed lobster to the pan along with the flour paste, tomato purée, sherry, cream, nutmeg and salt and pepper, to taste. Mix well.
5 Add the tarragon and remaining stock and cook, stirring continuously,

over high heat until the soup boils and thickens. Reduce the heat and simmer gently for 5 minutes. Season to taste and serve garnished with the reserved lobster and some sprigs of tarragon, if you want.

NUTRITION PER SERVE
Protein 30 g; Fat 35 g; Carbohydrate 20 g; Dietary Fibre 4 g; Cholesterol 220 mg; 2080 kJ (500 cal)

Lift the meat out of the lobster shells and lightly crush the shells with a mallet.

Add the puréed lobster, flour paste, tomato purée, sherry, cream and nutmeg.

Add the chopped tarragon and remaining stock to the pan.

GRILLED CAPSICUM SOUP WITH HERB OMELETTE

Preparation time: 20 minutes
Total cooking time: 50 minutes
Serves 4–6

1 yellow or green capsicum, quartered
4 red capsicums, quartered
1 tablespoon olive oil
1 red onion, chopped
1 clove garlic, crushed
1 potato, diced
2/3 cup (170 ml/5¹/2 fl oz) tomato juice
1 tablespoon balsamic vinegar

Herb omelette
3 eggs, lightly beaten
1 tablespoon milk
2 tablespoons chopped parsley
2 teaspoons oil
3 spring onions, finely chopped

1 Grill the capsicums skin-side-up under a hot grill until blackened. Place in a plastic bag and cool. Peel away the skin and dice the yellow and one of the red capsicums. Set aside the remaining red capsicum.

2 Heat the oil and cook the onion, stirring, over medium heat until transparent. Add the garlic and potato and cook, stirring, for 1 minute. Add the tomato juice and 3 cups (750 ml) water, bring to the boil, reduce the heat and cover. Simmer for 25 minutes, or until the potato is tender.

3 Blend the soup until smooth, in batches, with the reserved red capsicum. Return to the pan and add the diced capsicum, vinegar and seasoning. Reheat gently to serve.

4 To make the herb omelette, whisk the eggs, milk and parsley and season. Heat the oil in a frying pan. Add the spring onion and cook until just soft. Pour in the egg mixture and cook over moderate heat until set. Cool on a wire rack and cut into diamonds. Serve on top of the soup.

NUTRITION PER SERVE (6)
Protein 8 g; Fat 8 g; Carbohydrate 10 g; Dietary Fibre 3 g; Cholesterol 90 mg; 620 kJ (150 cal)

Dice the yellow capsicum and one of the red ones.

Add the reserved red capsicum to the blender or food processor.

It is best to use a non-stick frying pan, if you have one.

HOT BEEF BORSCHT

Preparation time: 30 minutes
Total cooking time: 2 hours 50 minutes
Serves 4–6

500 g (1 lb) gravy beef, cut into
    large pieces
500 g (1 lb) fresh beetroot
1 onion, finely chopped
1 carrot, cut into short strips
1 parsnip, cut into short strips
1 cup (75 g/2¹/2 oz) finely
    shredded cabbage
sour cream and chopped chives,
    to serve

1 Put the beef in a large, heavy-based pan with 4 cups (1 litre) of water and bring slowly to the boil. Reduce the heat, cover and simmer for 1 hour. Skim the surface as required.
2 Cut the stems from the beetroot, wash well and place in a large, heavy-based pan with 4 cups (1 litre) of water. Bring to the boil, reduce the heat and simmer for 40 minutes, or until tender. Drain, reserving 1 cup (250 ml/8 fl oz) of the liquid. Cool, then peel and grate the beetroot.
3 Remove the meat from the stock, cool and dice. Skim any fat from the surface of the stock. Return the meat to the stock and add the onion, carrot, parsnip, beetroot and reserved liquid. Bring to the boil, reduce the heat, cover and simmer for 45 minutes.
4 Add the cabbage, stir and simmer for a further 15 minutes. Season to taste. Serve topped with the sour cream and chives.

NUTRITION PER SERVE (6)
Protein 20 g; Fat 10 g; Carbohydrate 10 g;
Dietary Fibre 5 g; Cholesterol 80 mg;
940 kJ (225 cal)

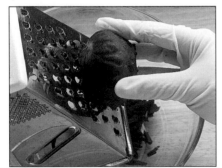

To avoid stains, wear rubber gloves to grate the beetroot.

Allow the meat to cool, then cut into dice using a sharp knife.

Pour the reserved beetroot liquid into the soup and bring to the boil.

SNOW PEA AND PRAWN SOUP

Preparation time: 10 minutes
Total cooking time: 25 minutes
Serves 4

350 g (11 oz) snow peas, topped
   and tailed
45 g (1¹/₂ oz) butter
1 leek, chopped
1 clove garlic, crushed
2 teaspoons grated fresh ginger
1¹/₂ tablespoons plain flour
4 cups (1 litre) chicken or fish
   stock (see page 82)
12 raw prawns, peeled,
   deveined and chopped
coriander leaves, to serve

1 Roughly chop the snow peas. Melt the butter in a large saucepan and add the leek, garlic and ginger. Cook over moderate heat until the leek is soft but not brown. Stir in the flour and cook for 1 minute.

2 Remove the pan from the heat and gradually stir in the stock. Return to the heat and bring to the boil, stirring continuously, until the mixture thickens slightly. Reduce the heat, cover the pan and simmer for 5 minutes. Add the snow peas and simmer for 5 minutes.

3 Purée the soup in batches in a blender or food processor, until smooth. Return to a clean pan, bring to the boil and add the prawns. Simmer for 2 minutes, or until the prawns turn pink and are cooked through.

4 Season to taste with salt and freshly ground black pepper. Serve immediately, sprinkled with fresh coriander leaves.

NUTRITION PER SERVE
Protein 17 g; Fat 10 g; Carbohydrate 8 g; Dietary Fibre 5 g; Cholesterol 110 mg; 780 kJ (185 cal)

COOK'S FILE

Hint: If you have one, it is best to purée this soup in a blender rather than a food processor. A food processor will give the soup a slightly granular and inferior texture.
Serving suggestion: This soup goes very well with the Ricotta and dill buns on page 94.

Starting from the tail end, pull the string from the snow peas and trim the tops.

Remove the heads, then peel away the shell from the body and tail of the prawn.

OSSO BUCO, BARLEY AND VEGETABLE SOUP

Preparation time: 25 minutes
Total cooking time: 50 minutes
Serves 6

500 g (1 lb) veal shanks with
    bones (osso buco), cut into
    5 cm (2 inch) pieces
    (ask your butcher to do this)
2 tablespoons olive oil
1 onion, diced
1–2 garlic cloves, crushed
425 g (14 oz) can chopped
    tomatoes
1 tablespoon tomato paste
1/2 teaspoon dried oregano
6 cups (1.5 litres) beef stock,
    (see page 82)
300 g (10 oz) potatoes, cubed
300 g (10 oz) pumpkin, cubed
3/4 cup (165 g/51/2 oz) pearl
    barley
200 g (61/2 oz) zucchini, sliced

1 Trim the meat from the bones and cut into cubes. Scrape out the marrow from the bones, if you want to use it, and discard the bones. Heat the oil in a heavy-based pan and brown the meat and marrow, in batches if necessary, until rich brown. Remove and drain on paper towels. Set the fried marrow aside, to garnish.

2 Add the onion to the pan and cook for 4–5 minutes over low heat; then add the garlic and cook for 1 minute longer. Add the meat, tomato, tomato paste, oregano, stock, potato and pumpkin.

3 Wash the barley in a sieve until the water runs clean, then drain and add to the soup. Bring to the boil, reduce the heat to low and simmer, covered, for 20 minutes. Add the zucchini and cook, covered, for 10 minutes, or until the barley is cooked. Serve garnished with the fried marrow.

NUTRITION PER SERVE
Protein 25 g; Fat 10 g; Carbohydrate 30 g; Dietary Fibre 6 g; Cholesterol 70 mg; 1310 kJ (315 cal)

COOK'S FILE

Note: Osso buco (or *ossobuco*) is the Italian for marrowbone. It is a stew made with the knuckle of veal, usually served in a tomato sauce.

Trim the meat from the bones and cut into cubes.

Add the meat, tomato, tomato paste, oregano, stock, potato and pumpkin.

Wash the barley in a sieve under running water until the water runs clear.

Add the zucchini to the boiling soup and cook for 10 minutes.

ROASTED VEGETABLE SOUP

Preparation time: 30 minutes
Total cooking time: 1 hour 35 minutes
Serves 6

2 carrots, cut into large pieces
1 parsnip, cut into large pieces
500 g (1 lb) unpeeled pumpkin, cut into large pieces
350 g (11 oz) unpeeled sweet potato, cut into large pieces
1 red capsicum, cut into large pieces
2 onions, halved
4 cloves garlic, unpeeled
3 cups (750 ml/24 fl oz) vegetable stock (see page 83)
sour cream and thyme, to serve

1 Preheat the oven to moderate 180°C (350°F/Gas 4). Put the vegetables in a large greased baking dish and brush lightly with some olive oil.

2 Bake for 1 hour, turning often. Remove the capsicum. Bake for 30 minutes longer; cool the vegetables slightly. Remove the skin from the capsicum; place in a food processor with the carrot, parsnip and onion.

3 Scrape the pumpkin and sweet potato flesh into the processor and squeeze in the garlic pulp. Add half the stock and puree until smooth. Place in a pan with the remaining stock and heat through. Season and serve with sour cream and thyme.

NUTRITION PER SERVE
Protein 3 g; Fat 5 g; Carbohydrate 20 g; Dietary Fibre 4 g; Cholesterol 4 mg; 540 kJ (130 cal)

COOK'S FILE

Serving suggestion: Serve with the Bacon, cheese and onion quickbread on page 110.

Cut the carrots, parnsip, pumpkin and sweet potato into large pieces.

Using your fingers, carefully peel away the blackened capsicum skin.

Using a teaspoon, scrape the flesh from the sweet potato and pumpkin.

Stir-ins

Quick and easy to make, these vegetarian stir-ins are a fabulous way to dress up your soups. Serve them on the table for diners to help themselves, or add a generous dollop to each bowl when you're dishing up. Either way, they turn a simple bowl of soup into something quite special.

SPICED CARROT PUREE

Melt 50 g (1¾ oz) butter in a medium pan. Peel and finely chop 500 g (1 lb) carrots and add to the butter, stirring until they are well coated. Add 1 teaspoon each ground cumin and coriander, ½ teaspoon ground cinnamon and a pinch each of ground cloves and nutmeg. Cook over medium heat for 3–4 minutes. Cover and cook for a further 10 minutes. Remove the lid, add ½ cup (125 ml/4 fl oz) vegetable stock and simmer for 15 minutes. Place the carrots and the liquid into a blender and blend until smooth. Season to taste with salt and freshly cracked pepper. Shown here with Lentil and spinach soup (page 18), but also delicious with French onion or most meat soups. Serves 6.

NUTRITION PER SERVE
Protein 1 g; Fat 7 g; Carbohydrate 5 g; Dietary Fibre 2 g; Cholesterol 20 mg; 350 kJ (80 cal)

ROUILLE

Cut 1 large red capsicum in half and remove the seeds and white membrane. Place skin-side-up under a preheated hot grill. Cook for 5 minutes, or until the skin has charred and blackened. Place in a plastic bag and allow to cool, then peel away the skin. Roughly chop and place in a food processor. Cut 1 potato into cubes. Cook until tender and, while still warm, place in the food processor with 2 chopped cloves garlic and 1 egg yolk. Process until smooth. With the motor running, gradually pour in ½ cup (125 ml/4 fl oz) olive oil in a thin stream, until you have a thick mixture. Shown here with Bouillabaisse (page 7), but also good with most fish soups. Serves 6.

NUTRITION PER SERVE
Protein 2 g; Fat 2 g; Carbohydrate 4 g; Dietary Fibre 1 g; Cholesterol 30 mg; 900 kJ (205 cal)

From left to right: Spiced carrot purée; Rouille;
Aïoli; Rocket and sun-dried tomato pesto;
Coriander pesto; Yoghurt and herb stir-in

AIOLI

Crush 6–8 cloves garlic and place in a food processor. Add 2 egg yolks and a pinch of salt and process until well combined. With the motor running, very slowly add 1 cup (250 ml/8 fl oz) olive oil, in a thin stream. Shown here with Spicy tomato and chickpea soup (page 44). Serves 6.

NUTRITION PER SERVE
Protein 1 g; Fat 10 g; Carbohydrate 0 g; Dietary Fibre 1 g; Cholesterol 30 mg; 405 kJ (100 cal)

ROCKET AND SUN-DRIED TOMATO PESTO

Add 2 cups (70 g/2¼ oz) finely shredded rocket leaves to a food processor. Add 2 crushed cloves garlic and ½ cup (50 g/1¾ oz) finely grated Parmesan. Finely chop ¼ cup (35 g/1¼ oz) sun-dried tomatoes and add to the rocket. Process until finely chopped. Add ¼ cup (60 ml/2 fl oz) olive oil and process again until well combined. Shown here with Roasted tomato soup (page 32), but good with most vegetable soups. Serves 6.

NUTRITION PER SERVE
Protein 3 g; Fat 10 g; Carbohydrate 0 g; Dietary Fibre 0 g; Cholesterol 8 mg; 515 kJ (120 cal)

CORIANDER PESTO

Place 2 cups (100 g/3½ oz) chopped coriander leaves and stems into a food processor. Finely chop 3 cloves garlic and add to the processor along with ½ cup (50 g/1¾ oz) grated Parmesan and a pinch of salt. Process until finely chopped. With the motor running, gradually add ¼ cup (60 ml/ 2 fl oz) olive oil, processing until all the ingredients are combined. Shown here with Spring vegetable soup (page 35), and good with vegetable broths. Serves 6.

NUTRITION PER SERVE
Protein 3 g; Fat 10 g; Carbohydrate 0 g; Dietary Fibre 0 g; Cholesterol 8 mg; 510 kJ (122 cal)

YOGHURT AND HERB STIR-IN

Combine ¾ cup (185 g/6 oz) thick natural yoghurt with 2 cloves crushed garlic, 3 tablespoons finely chopped mint and 2 tablespoons finely chopped coriander. Stir through 1 tablespoon lemon juice and season well. Add a generous spoonful to Borscht, Mulligatawny or Roast pumpkin soup (page 25), as shown here. Serves 6.

NUTRITION PER SERVE
Protein 2 g; Fat 1 g; Carbohydrate 2 g; Dietary Fibre 0 g; Cholesterol 5 mg; 100 kJ (25 cal)

MINESTRONE PRIMAVERA

Preparation time: 15 minutes
Total cooking time: 40 minutes
Serves 4–6

1/4 cup (60 ml/2 fl oz) olive oil
45 g (1 1/2 oz) pancetta, finely
    chopped
2 onions, chopped
2 cloves garlic, thinly sliced
2 small sticks celery, sliced
8 cups (2 litres) chicken stock
    (see page 82)
1/3 cup (50 g/1 3/4 oz) macaroni

2 zucchini, chopped
2 cups (150 g/5 oz) shredded
    savoy cabbage
1 1/2 cups (185 g/6 oz) green
    beans, chopped
1 cup (155 g/5 oz) frozen peas
1 cup (40 g/1 1/4 oz) shredded
    English spinach leaves
1/4 cup (15 g/1/2 oz) chopped
    basil
grated Parmesan, to serve

1 Put the oil, pancetta, onion, garlic and celery in a large pan and stir occasionally over low heat for 8 minutes, or until the vegetables are soft but not brown. Add the stock and bring to the boil. Simmer, covered, for 10 minutes.

2 Add the macaroni and boil for 12 minutes, or until almost tender. Stir in the zucchini, cabbage, beans and peas and simmer for 5 minutes. Add the spinach and basil and simmer for 2 minutes. Season to taste and serve with the grated Parmesan.

NUTRITION PER SERVE (6)
Protein 7 g; Fat 20 g; Carbohydrate 15 g;
Dietary Fibre 6 g; Cholesterol 40 mg;
1030 kJ (250 cal)

COOK'S FILE

Serving suggestion: Serve with the Savoury scroll on page 92.

Using a sharp knife, cut the pancetta into strips then chop finely.

Chop the zucchini and finely shred the savoy cabbage.

Add the shredded spinach and basil to the soup.

COUNTRY LENTIL, BACON AND GARLIC SOUP

Preparation time: 35 minutes
Total cooking time: 1 hour 5 minutes
Serves 4–6

1/4 cup (60 ml/2 fl oz) olive oil
3 onions, finely chopped
6 cloves garlic, thinly sliced
150 g (5 oz) speck or bacon, finely chopped
3 carrots, finely chopped
2 parsnips, finely chopped
3 sticks celery, sliced
200 g (6½ oz) red lentils, rinsed
4 cups (1 litre) vegetable stock (see page 83)
1/4 cup (60 g/2 oz) tomato paste
1/1 cup (65 g/2¼ oz) risoni (rice-shaped pasta)
4 spring onions, finely chopped
1/4 cup (15 g/½ oz) chopped parsley
2 teaspoons finely grated lemon rind
100 g (3½ oz) grated Parmesan, to serve

1 Heat the oil in a large pan. Add the onion, garlic and speck and cook, stirring occasionally, over low–medium heat for 15 minutes, or until a deep golden brown.
2 Add the carrot, parsnip and celery, stir well, cover and cook for 5 minutes, or until softened. Stir in the lentils, stock, tomato paste and 4 cups (1 litre) of water. Bring to the boil, reduce the heat and simmer, uncovered, for 30 minutes, or until the lentils are tender; skim the surface as required.
3 Stir in the risoni and 2 cups (500 ml/16 fl oz) of water. Return to the boil and simmer for 10 minutes.
4 Add the spring onion, parsley and lemon rind and season to taste. Serve with the grated Parmesan.

NUTRITION PER SERVE (6)
Protein 25 g; Fat 20 g; Carbohydrate 30 g; Dietary Fibre 10 g; Cholesterol 30 mg; 1590 kJ (380 cal)

COOK'S FILE

Serving suggestion: This soup goes very well with the Parmesan and prosciutto loaf on page 87.

Using a sharp knife, slice the garlic and finely chop the speck.

Add the well-drained lentils to the pan and stir well to combine.

CREAM OF ASPARAGUS SOUP

Preparation time: 20 minutes
Total cooking time: 55 minutes
Serves 4–6

1 kg (2 lb) asparagus spears
30 g (1 oz) butter
1 onion, finely chopped
1 litre (4 cups) chicken stock
    (see page 82)
1/4 cup (7 g/1/4 oz) basil leaves,
    chopped
1 teaspoon celery salt
1 cup (250 ml/8 fl oz) cream

1 Break off the woody ends from the asparagus and trim off the tips. Blanch the tips in boiling water for 1–2 minutes, refresh in cold water and set aside. Chop the remaining asparagus spears into large pieces.
2 Melt the butter in a large pan and cook the onion for 3–4 minutes over medium-low heat, or until soft and golden. Add the asparagus spears and cook for 1–2 minutes, stirring continuously.
3 Add the chicken stock, basil and celery salt. Bring to the boil, reduce the heat and simmer gently, covered, for 30 minutes.
4 Check that the asparagus is well cooked and soft. If not, simmer for a further 10 minutes. Set aside and allow to cool slightly.
5 Pour into a processor and process in batches until smooth. Then sieve into a clean pan. Return to the heat, pour in the cream and gently reheat. Do not allow the soup to boil. Season to taste with salt and white pepper.
6 Serve immediately, with the asparagus tips placed on top of the soup.

NUTRITION PER SERVE (6)
Protein 6 g; Fat 26 g; Carbohydrate 5 g; Dietary Fibre 3 g; Cholesterol 80 mg; 1130 kJ (270 cal)

COOK'S FILE

Hint: If you are not using home-made stock, always taste before adding seasoning to your soup—shop-bought stock can be very salty.
Serving suggestion: This soup goes very well with the White dinner rolls on page 90.

Break off the woody ends from the asparagus spears.

Test whether the asparagus is well cooked by piercing it with a fork.

NEW ENGLAND CLAM CHOWDER

Preparation time: 25 minutes
Total cooking time: 45 minutes
Serves 4

30 g (1 oz) butter
2 rashers bacon, finely chopped
1 large onion, finely chopped
4 potatoes, cut into 1 cm
    (1/2 inch) cubes
2 cups (500 ml/16 fl oz) fish
    stock (see page 83)
1 bay leaf
1/2 cup (125 ml/4 fl oz) milk

4 x 105 g (3 1/2 oz) cans baby
    clams, drained and chopped
1/4 cup (15 g/1/2 oz) finely
    chopped parsley
1 cup (250 ml/8 fl oz) cream

1 Heat the butter in a large pan. Cook the bacon and onion for 2–3 minutes, or until softened. Add the potato and stir. Cook for a further 2–3 minutes and gradually pour on the stock. Add the bay leaf.
2 Bring to the boil, reduce the heat and simmer, covered, for 20 minutes, or until the potato is cooked. Simmer for a further 10 minutes, or until the soup is reduced and slightly thickened. Remove the bay leaf and discard.
3 Add the milk, chopped clams, parsley and cream. Stir to reheat, but do not allow the soup to boil. Season to taste with salt and freshly ground black pepper.

NUTRITION PER SERVE
Protein 20 g; Fat 40 g; Carbohydrate 20 g; Dietary Fibre 3 g; Cholesterol 250 mg; 2090 kJ (500 cal)

COOK'S FILE

Note: New England clam chowder is one of the many types to come from the north-east of America—it is, of course, named after the state.

Peel and cut the potatoes into strips then small cubes.

Remove the bay leaf with a pair of tongs or a spoon.

Add the milk, clams and parsley and pour in the cream.

CUBAN BLACK BEAN SOUP

Preparation time: 20 minutes
+ overnight soaking
Total cooking time: 1 hour 40 minutes
Serves 6

2 cups (440 g/14 oz) dried black
    beans (see Note)
2 tablespoons oil
1 onion, sliced
2 teaspoons ground cumin
1 teaspoon ground coriander
1/2 teaspoon chilli powder
2 cloves garlic, crushed
300 g (10 oz) bacon bones
2 tablespoons red wine vinegar

1 tablespoon soft brown sugar
3 spring onions, chopped
1 tablespoon chopped parsley
2 hard-boiled eggs, chopped

1 Soak the black beans in plenty of cold water overnight. Drain.
2 Heat the oil in a large, heavy-based pan and cook the onion over medium heat for 5 minutes, or until softened. Add the cumin, coriander, chilli powder and garlic to the pan and cook for 1 minute.
3 Add the bacon bones and 5 cups (1.2 litres) of water, stirring well. Add the beans and bring to the boil; reduce the heat and simmer, partially covered, for 1–1½ hours, or until the beans are very soft.

4 Using a pair of tongs, remove the bacon bones from the pan and discard. Stir in the vinegar and sugar and season to taste. If you want a thicker soup, mash the beans slightly with a potato masher. Garnish with the spring onion, parsley and hard-boiled egg.

NUTRITION PER SERVE
Protein 20 g; Fat 9 g; Carbohydrate 30 g; Dietary Fibre 15 g; Cholesterol 70 mg; 1195 kJ (285 cal)

COOK'S FILE

Note: Black beans are also known as black turtle beans or Mexican black beans and are available at good delicatessens. They are not to be confused with Chinese black beans.

Add all the spices and crush the garlic into the pan.

The beans should be soft when crushed with a fork.

Remove the bacon bones from the pan with a pair of tongs.

BARLEY SOUP WITH GOLDEN PARSNIPS

Preparation time: 30 minutes
 + overnight soaking
Total cooking time: 2 hours 20 minutes
Serves 6

200 g (6¹/2 oz) pearl barley
1 tablespoon oil
2 onions, chopped
2 cloves garlic, finely chopped
2 carrots, chopped
2 potatoes, chopped
2 sticks celery, chopped
2 bay leaves, torn in half
8 cups (2 litres) chicken stock
 (see page 82)

¹/2 cup (125 ml/4 fl oz) milk
40 g (1¹/4 oz) butter
3 parsnips, cubed
1 teaspoon soft brown sugar
chopped parsley, to serve

1 Soak the barley in water overnight. Drain. Place in a saucepan with 8 cups (2 litres) of water. Bring to the boil, reduce the heat and simmer, partially covered, for 1 hour 15 minutes, or until tender. Drain.

2 Heat the oil in a large saucepan, add the chopped onion, garlic, carrot, potato and celery and cook for 3 minutes. Stir well and cook, covered, for 15 minutes over low heat, stirring occasionally.

3 Add the barley, bay leaves, chicken stock, milk and 2 teaspoons of salt and 1 teaspoon of pepper. Bring to the boil, then reduce the heat and simmer the soup, partially covered, for 35 minutes. If it is too thick, add cold water (about 1 cup/250 ml/8 fl oz), a little at a time, until the soup reaches your preferred consistency.

4 While the soup is simmering, melt the butter in a frying pan, add the parsnip and toss in the butter. Sprinkle with the sugar and cook until golden brown and tender. Serve the parsnip on top of the soup and sprinkle with the parsley.

NUTRITION PER SERVE
Protein 7 g; Fat 10 g; Carbohydrate 40 g; Dietary Fibre 8 g; Cholesterol 20 mg; 1190 kJ (285 cal)

Using a sharp knife, chop the potatoes, carrots and celery.

Add the drained barley to the cooked vegetables and stir in.

Sprinkle the soft brown sugar over the parsnip in the frying pan.

59

SAFFRON AND MUSSEL SOUP

Preparation time: 15 minutes
Total cooking time: 35 minutes
Serves 4

500 g (1 lb) mussels
1 stick celery, chopped
1 carrot, chopped
1 onion, chopped
3 black peppercorns
3–4 parsley stalks
100 g (3½ oz) butter, softened
10 spring onions, finely chopped
⅔ cup (40 g/1¼ oz) finely
    chopped parsley
2 cloves garlic, crushed

¾ cup (185 ml/6 fl oz) dry
    white wine
⅓ cup (40 g/1¼ oz) plain flour
1 cup (250 ml/8 fl oz) cream
pinch of saffron threads

1 To make the mussel stock, scrub the mussels, remove their beards and discard any open mussels. Place the mussels, celery, carrot, onion, peppercorns and parsley stalks in a pan with 6 cups (1.5 litres) of water and bring to the boil. Reduce the heat to low and simmer, covered, for 6 minutes.

2 Discard any unopened mussels. Strain the stock through a sieve lined with 2 layers of damp muslin. Rinse out the pan and reserve the mussels.

Return the stock to the pan and simmer for 15 minutes. Set aside.

3 Melt half the butter in a pan, add the spring onion and cook over moderate heat for 3–4 minutes, or until softened. Add the parsley, garlic and wine and season well with salt and freshly ground black pepper.

4 Mix the flour and remaining butter to a paste. Add the reserved stock to the pan and stir in the flour paste, cream and saffron threads, stir until the soup boils and thickens slightly. Simmer for 2–3 minutes. Add the mussels and stir gently until reheated.

NUTRITION PER SERVE
Protein 25 g; Fat 55 g; Carbohydrate 15 g;
Dietary Fibre 4 g; Cholesterol 290 mg;
2870 kJ (690 cal)

Discard any unopened mussels with a pair of tongs.

Strain the stock through a sieve lined with damp muslin over a bowl.

Saffron is expensive, but only a pinch is needed to give the colour and flavour.

CREAM OF BROCCOLI SOUP

Preparation time: 15 minutes
Total cooking time: 25 minutes
Serves 4–6

750 g (1 1/2 lb) broccoli
2 1/2 cups (600 ml/20 fl oz)
   chicken stock (see page 82)
pinch of nutmeg
1 cup (250 ml/8 fl oz) cream

1 Cut the broccoli stems and florets into chunks. Place in a large pan with 1 cup (250 ml/8 fl oz) of the stock, cover and bring to the boil. Reduce the heat to low and simmer, covered, for 10 minutes, or until the broccoli is tender. Stir occasionally.
2 Transfer half the mixture to a food processor and process until finely chopped. Add a little of the remaining stock and blend to a purée. Return to a pan.
3 Transfer the remaining broccoli mixture and stock to the food processor and process until finely chopped. Return all the puréed soup to the pan, add the nutmeg and cream and stir over moderate heat until heated through, but do not allow the soup to boil. Before serving, season to taste with salt and freshly ground black pepper.

NUTRITION PER SERVE (6)
Protein 7 g; Fat 20 g; Carbohydrate 2 g; Dietary Fibre 5 g; Cholesterol 60 mg; 825 kJ (200 cal)

COOK'S FILE

Serving suggestion: Try with the Zucchini and olive bread on page 93.
Variation: Use vegetable stock for a vegetarian meal.

Using a sharp knife, cut the broccoli stems and florets into chunks.

Process the broccoli mixture until finely chopped, then add a little stock.

Add a pinch of nutmeg and pour on the cream, stirring until heated through.

ROASTED APPLE AND PUMPKIN SOUP

Preparation time: 20 minutes
Total cooking time: 1 hour 30 minutes
Serves 4

2 red apples, unpeeled
¼ cup (60 ml/2 fl oz) olive oil
1 onion, finely chopped
2 teaspoons ground cumin
¼ teaspoon chilli powder
1 kg (2 lb) butternut pumpkin,
    roughly chopped
2 potatoes, chopped
2 teaspoons plain flour
4 cups (1 litre) vegetable stock
    (see page 83)
1¼ cups (315 ml/10 fl oz)
    cream

1 Preheat the oven to moderately hot 200°C (400°F/Gas 6). Cut the unpeeled apples into thick wedges and cut away the core. Lay in a baking dish and pour over 1 tablespoon of the oil. Roast for 25–30 minutes, turning occasionally, until golden brown. Set aside.

2 Heat the remaining oil in a large pan, add the onion, cumin and chilli and cook for 10 minutes over low heat, or until the onion is very soft and golden. Add the pumpkin and potato and cook for 15 minutes, over medium-high heat, tossing regularly, or until slightly brown. Add the flour and cook, stirring, for 1 minute.

3 Remove from the heat and gradually pour in the stock, stirring. Return to the heat, bring to the boil, then reduce the heat and simmer, covered, for 30 minutes. Drain, reserving the vegetables and stock.

4 Set aside 8 pieces of the roasted apple. Put the rest in a food processor, with half the vegetables and 1 cup (250 ml/8 fl oz) of the reserved stock. Purée until smooth and return to the pan. Repeat with the remaining vegetables and the same amount of stock; add to the pan with any remaining stock and the cream. Reheat and season well. Serve the remaining roasted apple as a garnish.

NUTRITION PER SERVE
Protein 9 g; Fat 50 g; Carbohydrate 40 g; Dietary Fibre 5 g; Cholesterol 105 mg; 2700 kJ (645 cal)

Using a sharp knife, seed and roughly chop the pumpkin.

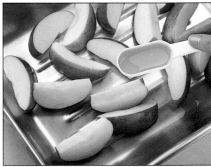

Lay the unpeeled apples in the baking tray and drizzle with the olive oil.

Cook the vegetables until they begin to brown a little.

Add some of the reserved stock to the vegetables and apple.

PASTA AND WHITE BEAN SOUP

Preparation time: 30 minutes
Total cooking time: 20 minutes
Serves 6

⅓ cup (50 g/1¾ oz) pine nuts
1 cup (50 g/1¾ oz) basil leaves
50 g (1¾ oz) rocket leaves
2 cloves garlic, chopped
⅓ cup (35 g/1¼ oz) finely
    grated Parmesan
⅓ cup (80 ml/2¾ fl oz) olive
    oil
185 g (6 oz) spiral pasta

6 cups (1.5 litres) chicken
    stock (see page 82)
2 x 300 g (10 oz) cans
    cannellini beans, drained

1 Put the pine nuts in a frying pan and dry fry them over moderate heat for 1–2 minutes, or until golden brown. Remove from the pan and allow to cool.

2 To make the pesto, mix the pine nuts, basil, rocket, garlic and Parmesan in a food processor and process until finely chopped. With the motor running, add the oil in a thin stream until well combined. Season to taste with salt and pepper. Set aside.

3 Cook the pasta until just underdone. Heat the chicken stock in a large pan until it begins to boil. Reduce the heat to simmering point. Drain the pasta and add to the stock with the cannellini beans. Reheat and serve with a spoonful of pesto.

NUTRITION PER SERVE
Protein 15 g; Fat 20 g; Carbohydrate 40 g; Dietary Fibre 4 g; Cholesterol 5 mg; 1770 kJ (425 cal)

COOK'S FILE

Note: Cannellini beans are small, white and slightly kidney-shaped and are used a lot in Italian cooking, particularly in Tuscany.

Dry fry the pine nuts until golden brown, but take care not to let them burn.

Put the pine nuts, basil, rocket, garlic and Parmesan in a food processor.

Add the drained cannellini beans to the simmering stock.

ORANGE-SCENTED, CURRIED PARSNIP SOUP

Preparation time: 25 minutes
Total cooking time: 40 minutes
Serves 6–8

50 g (1³/4 oz) butter
1 onion, chopped
800 g (1 lb 10 oz) parsnips, diced
2 teaspoons curry powder
¹/3 cup (80 ml/2³/4 fl oz) orange juice

¹/2 teaspoon grated orange rind
6 cups (1.5 litres) chicken stock (see page 82)
strips of orange rind, to garnish

1 Melt the butter in a large pan. Cook the onion for 2–3 minutes, then stir in the parsnip. Cover the pan and cook over low heat, stirring occasionally, for 20 minutes, or until the parsnip has softened but not browned.
2 Add the curry powder and cook for a further 2–3 minutes. Add the orange juice and rind. Put the parsnip mixture in a blender and blend in batches until smooth. Return to the pan and pour on the stock. Bring to the boil and simmer for 15 minutes.
3 Season to taste and garnish with the orange rind. Serve with a spoonful of cream stirred through the soup.

NUTRITION PER SERVE (8)
Protein 2 g; Fat 5 g; Carbohydrate 10 g; Dietary Fibre 3 g; Cholesterol 15 mg; 445 kJ (105 cal)

COOK'S FILE

Serving suggestion: Both soups shown are delicious served with the Mini bagels on page 97.

Peel and cut the parsnips into strips then finely dice.

Peel the orange rind, remove the white pith, then cut the rind into thin strips.

Add the curry powder to the onion and parsnip and mix in well.

POTATO, PEA AND PARMESAN SOUP

Preparation time: 45 minutes
Total cooking time: 1 hour
Serves 4

750 g (1¹/2 lb) unshelled peas
¹/4 cup (60 ml/2 fl oz) olive oil
30 g (1 oz) butter
3 cloves garlic, thinly sliced
2 onions, very thinly sliced
500 g (1 lb) potatoes, chopped
2 teaspoons plain flour

2 cups (500 ml/16 fl oz) beef stock (see page 82)
2 teaspoons grated lemon rind
¹/4 cup (15 g/¹/2 oz) chopped flat-leaf parsley
¹/2 cup (125 ml/4 fl oz) cream
100 g (3¹/2 oz) grated Parmesan

1 Shell the peas and set aside.
2 Heat the oil and butter in a large, heavy-based pan. Add the garlic, onion and potato and cook, stirring regularly, for 15–20 minutes, or until the potato is golden. Add the flour and stir for 2 minutes. Add the stock and 3 cups (750 ml/24 fl oz) of water and bring to the boil, stirring until the mixture thickens slightly. Reduce the heat and simmer, covered, for 20 minutes.
3 Add the peas, lemon rind and parsley. Simmer for 10 minutes, or until the peas are just tender. Stir in the cream, half the Parmesan and season to taste. Serve the remaining Parmesan with the soup.

NUTRITION PER SERVE
Protein 25 g; Fat 40 g; Carbohydrate 40 g; Dietary Fibre 15 g; Cholesterol 90 mg; 2650 kJ (630 cal)

Using a sharp knife, slice the garlic and onion very thinly.

Cook the onion, garlic and potato until golden brown, stirring regularly.

Stir in the peas, grated lemon rind and chopped parsley.

Orange-scented, curried parsnip soup (top) with Potato, pea and Parmesan soup

HEARTY MINESTRONE

Preparation time: 30 minutes
Total cooking time: 1 hour 25 minutes
Serves 6–8

2 tablespoons olive oil
2 onions, chopped
2 rashers bacon, chopped
1 potato, chopped into large
    cubes
280 g (9 oz) sweet potato,
    chopped into large cubes
3 carrots, sliced
250 g (8 oz) pumpkin, cubed
400 g (13 oz) cabbage, shredded
280 g (9 oz) yellow squash,
    sliced

220 g (7 oz) green beans,
    chopped
2 x 400 g (13 oz) can chopped
    tomatoes
6 cups (1.5 litres) chicken stock
    (see page 82)
1 teaspoon dried Italian herbs
1 teaspoon dried oregano
1/2 cup (80 g/2 3/4 oz) macaroni
300 g (10 oz) can butter beans
grated Parmesan, to serve

1 Heat the oil and cook the onion and bacon for 3–4 minutes over moderate heat, or until the onion is just brown. Reduce the heat slightly and add the potato and sweet potato. Stir and cook for 1–2 minutes. Add the carrot and pumpkin and cook for a further

1–2 minutes, stirring continuously.
2 Add the cabbage, squash, green beans, tomato, stock and herbs. Increase the heat and bring to the boil. Reduce the heat and simmer gently, covered, for 1 hour.
3 Add the macaroni and butter beans and cook for a further 10–12 minutes, or until the pasta is tender. Season to taste. Serve with the Parmesan.

NUTRITION PER SERVE (8)
Protein 9 g; Fat 6 g; Carbohydrate 30 g;
Dietary Fibre 8 g; Cholesterol 5 mg;
840 kJ (200 cal)

COOK'S FILE

Serving suggestion: This soup is traditionally served with Grissini, see page 95.

Slice the squash, chop the green beans and finely shred the cabbage.

Cook the onion and bacon until the onion is just brown.

Add the macaroni to the soup and cook until tender.

Fast Blender Tomato Soup

4 servings (makes 4 cups), Healthy

This creamy soup has a secret: There's no cream — or even butter — in it. Instead, bread and olive oil emulsify in the blender with the other ingredients to create a rich texture, making it easy to put together with a handful of pantry ingredients in just a few minutes.

The original recipe was made using a high-powered blender, such as a Vitamix, which has the capacity to both heat and blend the soup; it has been adapted here for a standard blender. You will just need to finish the soup on the stove after it's blended to allow the flavors to meld.

MAKE AHEAD: The soup can be refrigerated for up to 1 week.

Adapted from a recipe by J. Kenji Lopez-Alt, managing culinary director at SeriousEats.com.

Ingredients
- ⅓ cup olive oil
- 1 clove garlic
- ½ cup chopped onion
- 1 slice white or whole-wheat bread (crusts removed), torn into 1-inch pieces
- 28 ounces canned, no-salt-added whole peeled tomatoes, plus their juices
- 1 cup no-salt-added vegetable broth
- 1 teaspoon seasoning blend, such as Trader Joe's 21 Seasoning Salute
- Salt
- Freshly ground black pepper

Steps
- Combine the oil, garlic, onion, bread pieces, the tomatoes and their juices, the broth and seasoning blend in a blender; begin to blend on low, then gradually increase to high until pureed and smooth.
- Pour into a medium saucepan; cook over medium-low heat for 20 minutes, stirring a few times. Taste, and season with salt and pepper, as needed.
- Serve warm.

Nutrition | Per serving: 270 calories, 3 g protein, 22 g carbohydrates, 19 g fat, 3 g saturated fat, 0 mg cholesterol, 560 mg sodium, 4 g dietary fiber, 12 g sugar

BY KRISTEN HARTKE

You may have grown up in a home with cabinets full of random spice jars and multiple types of vinegar, oil and hot sauce; a freezer full of toaster pizzas and bison burgers; and a refrigerator groaning with fresh lettuce, five types of cheese and both yellow and brown mustard. But now that you're going off to college, you have nothing. And you may have to share your kitchen with at least three other people, so you'll need to focus on the essential items that can be mixed and matched to create new flavors with a minimum of ingredients.

Bottom line: You might not go grocery shopping very often, and it's a waste of money to buy a lot of fresh dairy, meat and produce that ends up rotting in the back of the refrigerator, so shelf-stable and frozen foods can give you the most bang for your buck — if you know how to make them tasty.

Spices, sauces and more

Besides salt and pepper, stock up on **ground cinnamon** and **ginger**, then add **curry powder**, **chili powder** and a **dried seasoning blend** such as Trader Joe's 21 Seasoning Salute. **Vanilla extract**, along with **honey**, **agave syrup** or **maple syrup**, brings a touch of sweetness to cookies, pancakes and yogurt. To add depth of flavor to soups, stews, casseroles and more, stock up on **olive oil**, **soy sauce**, **red wine vinegar**, **canned tomatoes** and **chicken or vegetable broth**, while **canned coconut milk** is a great shelf-stable substitute for dairy milk. **Panko bread crumbs** may seem like a nonessential item, but, when toasted in a pan with a little dried seasoning and salt, they make a delicious and crunchy topping for pasta when there's no Parmesan in the fridge. Rather than keep flour and baking powder, buy a **baking mix** such as Bisquick.

Protein staples

Beans are an essential part of

the most healthful diets around the world, so stock up on cans of **chickpeas** (garbanzo beans), **black beans** and **cannellini beans**, then add a bag of **dried brown lentils**, which can cook up to tender in just about 30 minutes. But the biggest secret weapon may be **raw cashews**, usually found in the natural-foods aisle of the grocery store. Not to be confused with roasted, salted cashews, which are found with peanuts and other snack foods, raw cashews can be boiled and then pureed with water in a blender to create a creamlike sauce, all in about 10 minutes flat. Because of its neutral flavor, cashew cream makes a great base for savory or sweet dishes, and a little goes a long way, so spending a little extra up front for the raw cashews will pay off in the end.

Stocking the freezer

Contrary to popular belief, fro-

zen fruits and ly are quite frozen shortly they retain ents. When bu avoid those th sonings or sa extra sodium on items such **peas, broccol** and **strawber** ful of peas int and lemon ze blueberry sco forting brocco

Meat, pou can be frozen properly. Firs fresh, then di into smaller defrost only defrost only **pork and lan** can be frozen while **frozen** used within t **fresh poult** breasts, etc.)

Using a vegetable peeler, peel the Jerusalem artichokes, then roughly chop.

Add the onion, artichoke and potato and cook over low heat.

Add the brandy and flour and cook for 1 minute.

Once the cream is added, season to taste with salt and freshly ground black pepper.

CREAM OF JERUSALEM ARTICHOKE SOUP

Preparation time: 45 minutes
Total cooking time: 30 minutes
Serves 4

50 g (1¾ oz) butter
2 onions, finely chopped
500 g (1 lb) Jerusalem
    artichokes, roughly chopped
2 potatoes, roughly chopped
1 tablespoon brandy
1 tablespoon plain flour
3 cups (750 ml/24 fl oz) chicken
    stock (see page 82)
¾ cup (185 ml/6 fl oz) cream
chopped parsley, to serve

1 Melt the butter in a large pan over medium heat until foamy. Add the onion, artichoke and potato and cook, covered, over low heat for 10 minutes. Uncover and cook, stirring regularly, for 8 minutes.

2 Stir in the brandy and flour, and cook for 1 minute. Gradually stir in about 2 cups (500 ml/16 fl oz) of the stock and cook, stirring continuously, until the soup boils and thickens. Simmer for a further 5 minutes. Transfer to a food processor and purée until smooth, adding more stock if needed.

3 Return to the pan, add the cream and season well with plenty of salt and freshly ground black pepper, then reheat. Sprinkle with the chopped parsley, to serve.

NUTRITION PER SERVE
Protein 7 g; Fat 30 g; Carbohydrate 20 g; Dietary Fibre 5 g; Cholesterol 100 mg; 1650 kJ (395 cal)

COOK'S FILE

Note: Jerusalem artichoke is a white-fleshed root related to the sunflower. It is not related to the thistle-like globe artichoke, even though they share the same name and taste rather similar.

CABBAGE AND HAM SOUP WITH CHEESE DUMPLINGS

Preparation time: 40 minutes
Total cooking time: 1 hour 10 minutes
Serves 6

1/4 cup (60 ml/2 fl oz) olive oil
350 g (11 oz) piece of Kasseler
  or double-smoked ham,
  chopped into cubes
2 teaspoons soft brown sugar
2 onions, thinly sliced
2 leeks, thinly sliced
3 cloves garlic, finely chopped
1 tablespoon plain flour
2 cups (500 ml/16 fl oz) chicken
  stock (see page 82)
250 g (8 oz) bacon bones
3 potatoes, chopped
1/2 savoy cabbage, finely
  shredded
1 tablespoon white wine vinegar

Cheese dumplings
30g (1 oz) cold butter, cut into
  small pieces
2 cups (250 g/8 oz) self-raising
  flour
60 g (2 oz) finely grated
  Cheddar
2 teaspoons finely chopped
  thyme
2 teaspoons finely grated lemon
  rind, optional

1 Heat 1 tablespoon of the oil in a large pan and add the ham and sugar. Sauté over high heat, stirring continuously, for 5 minutes, or until just golden. Remove with a slotted spoon and drain on paper towels. Take care not to overcook or the ham will become dry.

2 Add the remaining oil, onion, leek and garlic and cook for 15 minutes over low heat, stirring regularly. Add the flour and cook for 1 minute, stirring. Remove from the heat and gradually add the stock, bacon bones and 6 cups (1.5 litres) of water. Return to the heat and cook, stirring, until the mixture comes to the boil and thickens slightly. Reduce the heat and simmer for 30 minutes, skimming the surface as required.

3 Remove the bacon bones, cut off the meat and discard the bones. Shred the meat into small pieces. Return to the pan with the potato and simmer for 10 minutes, or until the potato is tender. Add the ham, cabbage and vinegar and season with pepper, cover and cook over very low heat for 5–10 minutes while preparing the dumplings.

4 To make the dumplings, rub the butter into the flour until crumbly. Mix in the Cheddar, thyme and about 1/2 cup (125 ml/4 fl oz) of water, or enough to bind the mixture together. Roll 2 level teaspoons of the mixture into balls. Place into the soup and simmer, covered, for 8 minutes, or until the dumplings are plump. Season to taste and scatter with the lemon rind. Serve immediately.

NUTRITION PER SERVE
Protein 20 g; Fat 20 g; Carbohydrate 47 g; Dietary Fibre 6 g; Cholesterol 53 mg; 1947 kJ (467 cal)

COOK'S FILE

Note: Kasseler ham is cured and smoked ham—a traditional German speciality.
Hint: Avoid crusty-looking bacon bones as they are extremely salty. Taste before adding any extra salt to this recipe.

Using a sharp knife, cut the ham into slices and then into cubes.

Remove the ham with a slotted spoon and drain on paper towels.

Add the water, stock and bacon bones to the pan.

Add the peeled chopped potato to the pan and simmer until tender.

With a flat-bladed knife, mix in the cheese and thyme, then add the water.

The dumplings are ready when they are plump and float to the surface.

CREAM OF MUSHROOM SOUP

Preparation time: 30 minutes
Total cooking time: 15 minutes
Serves 4

500 g (1 lb) large field mushrooms
50 g (1³/4 oz) butter
4 spring onions, finely chopped
3 cloves garlic, finely chopped
1 teaspoon chopped lemon thyme

2 teaspoons plain flour
4 cups (1 litre) chicken or vegetable stock (see page 83)
1 cup (250 ml/8 fl oz) cream
chives and thyme, to garnish

1 Thinly slice the mushroom caps, discarding the stalks. Melt the butter in a heavy-based pan and cook the spring onion, garlic and lemon thyme, stirring, for 1 minute, or until the garlic is golden. Add the mushroom and 1/2 teaspoon each of salt and white pepper. Cook for 3–4 minutes, or until the mushroom just softens. Add the flour and cook, stirring, for 1 minute.

2 Remove from the heat and add the stock, stirring continuously. Return to the heat and bring to the boil, stirring. Reduce the heat and simmer gently for 2 minutes, stirring occasionally.

3 Whisk the cream into the soup, then reheat gently, stirring. Do not allow the soup to boil. Season to taste with salt and pepper, and garnish with the chopped chives and thyme.

NUTRITION PER SERVE
Protein 8 g; Fat 50 g; Carbohydrate 6 g; Dietary Fibre 4 g; Cholesterol 190 mg; 1985 kJ (475 cal)

Pull the lemon thyme leaves from the stems and chop them.

Remove the stalks from the mushrooms and thinly slice the caps.

Whisk in the cream, then reheat the soup gently without boiling.

CAULIFLOWER SOUP WITH CHEDDAR FINGERS

Preparation time: 25 minutes
Total cooking time: 1 hour
Serves 4

20 g (³/4 oz) butter
1 onion, chopped
1 stick celery, chopped
1 potato, chopped
¹/2 teaspoon ground nutmeg
750 g (1¹/2 lb) cauliflower, cut
    into florets
4 cups (1 litre) chicken or
    vegetable stock
    (see page 82)
1 cup (250 ml/8 fl oz) cream

Cheddar fingers
4 slices white bread, crusts
    removed
20 g (³/4 oz) butter, melted
1 clove garlic, crushed
¹/2 cup (60 g/2 oz) finely grated
    Cheddar

1 Melt the butter in a large pan. Cook the onion for 1–2 minutes. Add the celery, potato and nutmeg. Cook, stirring, for a further 2–3 minutes, then add the cauliflower florets.

2 Pour on the stock and bring to the boil, then reduce the heat and simmer for 20 minutes, or until the vegetables are tender. Stir occasionally.

3 Place in a food processor in batches and process until smooth. Return to the pan, add the cream and season to taste. Reheat gently, but do not allow the soup to boil.

4 To make the Cheddar bread fingers, preheat the oven to moderate 180°C (350°F/Gas 4). Brush the bread on both sides with the combined butter and garlic. Cut each slice into 4 fingers. Lay on a baking tray and bake for 10 minutes, or until crisp. Sprinkle with the Cheddar and bake for a further 10 minutes, or until golden and the cheese has melted. Float two fingers on top of the soup for each person and serve the rest alongside.

NUTRITION PER SERVE
Protein 13 g; Fat 40 g; Carbohydrate 25 g; Dietary Fibre 5 g; Cholesterol 125 mg; 2190 kJ (520 cal)

Using a sharp knife, trim the cauliflower into florets.

Add the ground nutmeg to the pan and mix in with a wooden spoon.

Sprinkle the grated Cheddar onto the crisp bread fingers.

CHICKEN NOODLE SOUP

Preparation time: 15 minutes
+ 1 hour refrigeration
Total cooking time: 1 hour 20 minutes
Serves 4–6

1.25 kg (2¹/2 lb) chicken wings
2 sticks celery, chopped
1 carrot, chopped
1 onion, chopped
1 bay leaf
1 sprig thyme
4 parsley stalks
45 g (1¹/2 oz) dried fine egg
    noodles, gently crushed

250 g (8 oz) chicken breast
    fillets, finely chopped
2 tablespoons chopped parsley
chopped chives, to serve

1 To make the chicken stock, rinse the chicken wings and place in a large pan with the celery, carrot, onion, bay leaf, thyme, parsley stalks, 1 teaspoon salt and 8 cups (2 litres) of water. Bring to the boil slowly, skimming the surface as required. Simmer, covered, for 1 hour. Allow to cool slightly, then strain and discard the chicken and vegetables.
2 Cool the stock further, then cover and refrigerate for at least 1 hour, or

until fat forms on the surface and can be spooned off.
3 Place the stock in a large pan and bring to the boil. Add the noodles, return to the boil and simmer for 8 minutes, or until tender. Add the chopped chicken and parsley and simmer for a further 4–5 minutes. Serve topped with the chives.

NUTRITION PER SERVE (6)
Protein 45 g; Fat 8 g; Carbohydrate 8 g; Dietary Fibre 2 g; Cholesterol 135 mg; 1205 kJ (290 cal)

COOK'S FILE

Serving suggestion: This soup goes well with the Onion buns on page 102.

Using a skimmer or slotted spoon, skim the surface of the stock as required.

Using a spoon, remove the fat that forms on the surface of the chilled stock.

Add the crushed noodles, then simmer for 8 minutes, or until tender.

Using a fine strainer, drain the liquid from the crab meat.

Using a sharp knife, peel the ginger, cut into strips, then chop finely.

Fold over the wrapper to enclose the filling and press firmly.

Cut the spring onions into lengths, then into thin strips.

LARGE CRAB DUMPLING SOUP

Preparation time: 25 minutes
Total cooking time: 20 minutes
Serves 4

170 g (5½ oz) can crab meat, drained
2 tablespoons finely chopped spring onions
2 cloves garlic, finely chopped
2 teaspoons sesame oil
3 teaspoons chopped ginger
12 small gowgee or won ton wrappers
2 spring onions, extra
5 cups (1.25 litres) chicken stock (see page 82)
1 tablespoon soy sauce
1 tablespoon mirin (see Note)
1 teaspoon sugar

1 To make the crab filling, mix the crab with the spring onion, 1 clove of garlic, 1 teaspoon of sesame oil and 1 teaspoon of the ginger.

2 Place 2 teaspoons of filling on one half of each wrapper. Moisten the edge with some water and fold over to form a crescent. Press the edges together firmly. Lay the dumplings on a lightly floured surface.

3 Cut the extra spring onions into thin strips and set aside. Heat the remaining sesame oil in a pan, add the remaining garlic and ginger and cook over medium heat for 3–4 minutes, or until the garlic is lightly golden. Add the stock, soy sauce, mirin and sugar. Bring to the boil, add the spring onion strips and simmer for 2–3 minutes.

4 Bring a large pan of water to the boil, add 3–4 dumplings at a time and cook for 5 minutes, or until just cooked. Place in bowls, ladle the stock over the dumplings and serve.

NUTRITION PER SERVE
Protein 30 g; Fat 20 g; Carbohydrate 35 g; Dietary Fibre 5 g; Cholesterol 50 mg; 1800 kJ (430 cal)

COOK'S FILE

Note: Mirin is a Japanese sweetened rice wine which is used frequently in cooking.

CREAM OF CELERY SOUP

Preparation time: 40 minutes
Total cooking time: 25 minutes
Serves 4

2½ cups (600 ml/20 fl oz) milk
1 onion, studded with 3 cloves
1⅔ cups (410 ml/13 fl oz)
    vegetable stock
    (see page 83)
4 celery tops and leaves
2 bay leaves, torn in half
3 stalks celery
60 g (2 oz) butter
1 onion, finely chopped
¼ cup (30 g/1 oz) plain flour
½ cup (125 ml/4 fl oz) cream

Blue cheese croutons
4 slices bread
80 g (2¾ oz) blue cheese, at
    room temperature
40 g (1¼ oz) finely grated
    mozzarella cheese

1 Put the milk, studded onion, stock, celery tops and leaves, bay leaves and ½ teaspoon each of salt and white pepper in a pan. Bring to the boil, then reduce the heat and simmer gently for 8 minutes. Allow to cool, then strain. Set aside, discarding the flavourings.
2 Cut the celery into matchsticks. Heat the butter in a large pan and, when foaming, add the onion and cook for 5 minutes, or until softened. Add the celery and cook for a further 2 minutes. Add the flour and cook for 1 minute, stirring continuously.
3 Remove from the heat and gradually stir in the stock. Return to the heat and cook, stirring, until the mixture boils and thickens. Simmer for 2 minutes. Stir in the cream and season to taste. Set aside and keep warm.
4 To make the blue cheese croutons, lightly toast the bread, then trim away the crusts. Spread the bread with the blue cheese and sprinkle with the mozzarella. Grill for 1–2 minutes, or until golden. Cut into 8 triangles and float a couple on top of the soup. Serve the rest alongside.

NUTRITION PER SERVE
Protein 15 g; Fat 40 g; Carbohydrate 30 g;
Dietary Fibre 2 g; Cholesterol 125 mg;
2340 kJ (560 cal)

Peel the onion and stud with the cloves, pressing firmly to secure.

Using a sharp knife, cut the celery into even-sized lengths, then into matchsticks.

Remove the pan from the heat and pour in the stock.

Trim the crusts from the toasted bread and spread with the blue cheese.

LEMON CHICKEN SOUP

Preparation time: 10 minutes
Total cooking time: 10 minutes
Serves 4

2 chicken breast fillets
1 lemon
4 cups (1 litre) chicken stock
    (see page 82)
2 sprigs lemon thyme, plus
    extra, to garnish (see Note)

1 Trim any excess fat from the chicken. Using a vegetable peeler, cut 2 strips of rind from the lemon and remove the pith. Place the stock, rind and thyme in a shallow pan and slowly bring almost to the boil. Reduce to simmering point, add the chicken and cook, covered, for 7 minutes, or until the meat is tender.
2 Remove the chicken from the pan, transfer to a plate and cover with foil.
3 Strain the stock through a sieve lined with 2 layers of damp muslin into a clean pan. Finely shred the chicken and return to the stock. Reheat gently and season to taste with salt and freshly ground black pepper. Serve immediately, garnished with the extra sprigs of thyme.

NUTRITION PER SERVE
Protein 25 g; Fat 3 g; Carbohydrate 0 g; Dietary Fibre 0 g; Cholesterol 55 mg; 535 kJ (130 cal)

COOK'S FILE

Note: You can use ordinary thyme if lemon thyme is not available.
Hint: If you don't have time to make your own stock, poultry shops or butchers sometimes sell their own. These may have more flavour and contain less salt than stock cubes.

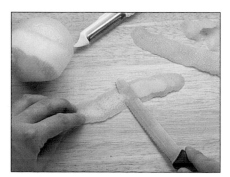

Using a small knife, remove the white pith from the lemon rind.

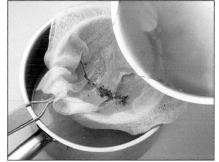

Pour the stock through a sieve lined with damp muslin into a clean pan.

Finely shred the chicken into thin pieces and return to the soup.

CHILLI, CHICKPEA AND CORIANDER SOUP

Preparation time: 20 minutes
Total cooking time: 25 minutes
Serves 2–4

30 g (1 oz) butter
1 onion, roughly chopped
3 cloves garlic, crushed
2 red chillies, seeded and finely
   chopped
2 teaspoons ground cumin
1 teaspoon ground turmeric
1 teaspoon ground coriander
425 g (14 oz) can chickpeas
1/3 cup (20 g/3/4 oz) chopped
   coriander leaves and stalks

1 teaspoon grated lemon rind
2 1/2 cups (600 ml/20 fl oz)
   chicken or vegetable stock
   (see page 82)

Crispy gremolata
2 slices of bread
30 g (1 oz) butter, melted
2 tablespoons chopped parsley
1 tablespoon grated lemon rind

1 Heat the butter in a large pan. Cook the onion, garlic and chilli for 2–3 minutes, or until softened but not browned. Add the spices and cook for 1–2 minutes, then add the chickpeas.
2 Process in a food processor until smooth. Add the coriander and lemon rind, pour on the stock and process until smooth. Reheat gently for 15 minutes, stirring frequently, but do not allow the soup to boil. Season to taste with salt and freshly ground black pepper.
3 To make the crispy gremolata, preheat the oven to moderate 180°C (350°F/Gas 4). Put the bread in a food processor and chop roughly. Lay the crumbs on a baking tray and mix in the butter. Bake for 5 minutes, or until crisp. Mix the parsley and lemon rind together and add to the gremolata just before serving. Serve the gremolata sprinkled on top of the soup.

NUTRITION PER SERVE (4)
Protein 20 g; Fat 20 g; Carbohydrate 50 g; Dietary Fibre 15 g; Cholesterol 40 mg; 1870 kJ (450 cal)

Using a sharp knife, chop the coriander leaves and stalks.

Add the ground cumin, turmeric and coriander to the pan.

Mix through the melted butter with the breadcrumbs on the baking tray.

POTATO AND GARLIC SOUP

Preparation time: 15 minutes
Total cooking time: 1 hour 5 minutes
Serves 4–6

2 bulbs garlic
500 g (1 lb) potatoes
2 tablespoons olive oil
1 onion, finely chopped
8 cups (2 litres) chicken stock
   (see page 82)
chopped chives, to serve

1 Separate the garlic bulbs into cloves and gently crush with the flat side of a knife to split the skin. Peel the cloves and cut in half. Chop the potatoes into small cubes.

2 Heat the olive oil in a large frying pan, add the onion and garlic and cook over medium-low heat for 5–10 minutes, or until the garlic is lightly golden. Add the potato and cook over low heat for 5 minutes. Add the chicken stock and simmer for 40–45 minutes, or until the garlic is very soft and the stock has reduced. Set aside to cool slightly.

3 Process the soup in batches in a food processor until smooth. Return to the pan and add 1/2 teaspoon of salt; taste before adding any more seasoning. Reheat gently before serving. Serve with a sprinkling of chopped chives.

NUTRITION PER SERVE (6)
Protein 3 g; Fat 7 g; Carbohydrate 15 g; Dietary Fibre 4 g; Cholesterol 0 mg; 540 kJ (130 cal)

COOK'S FILE

Note: If you don't have time to make stock, butchers or poultry shops may sell their own. Or try the carton stocks from supermarkets, which contain less salt and additives than cubes. If you are not using home-made stock, make sure you taste the soup before seasoning—some shop-bought stocks can be extremely salty. Season after cooking, as long simmering tends to concentrate the flavours of the soup.
Serving suggestion: Serve with the Walnut bread on page 101.

Two bulbs may seem a lot, but once it is cooked garlic takes on a mellow flavour.

Crush each clove with the flat side of a knife to split the skin.

Simmer the stock until the garlic cloves are very soft.

POTAGE BONNE FEMME

Preparation time: 20 minutes
Total cooking time: 45 minutes
Serves 6

30 g (1 oz) butter
1 tablespoon olive oil
2 leeks, thinly sliced
500 g (1 lb) potatoes, finely
    chopped
2 carrots, finely chopped
7 cups (1.75 litres) vegetable
    stock (see page 83)
finely chopped flat-leaf parsley,
    to garnish

1 Melt the butter and oil in a large pan. Add the leek and cook over low heat for 5 minutes, or until softened. Add the potato and carrot and cook over medium heat for 5 minutes, stirring continuously.
2 Add the stock and slowly bring to the boil. Simmer, covered, for 25–30 minutes, or until the vegetables are tender. Allow to cool slightly.
3 Process the soup in a food processor in batches until smooth and return to the pan. Reheat gently over low heat and season well with salt and freshly cracked pepper. Serve sprinkled with chopped parsley.

NUTRITION PER SERVE
Protein 5 g; Fat 8 g; Carbohydrate 20 g; Dietary Fibre 5 g; Cholesterol 13 mg; 650 kJ (160 cal)

COOK'S FILE

Hint: If you don't have time to make your own stock, ask your butcher or poultry shop if they make their own. Alternatively, buy supermarket stock in cartons—these tend to be less salty than the cubes.

When using shop-bought stock be careful with the amount of seasoning you add, as they can be rather salty. Always taste before seasoning.
Note: Potage Bonne Femme is an old-fashioned traditional French soup. *Potage* is the French word for soup and *bonne femme* (literally, 'good wife') is the term applied to dishes that are prepared in a simple, family or rustic fashion.
Serving suggestion: This soup goes very well with the Mini wholemeal loaves on page 86.

Thinly slice the leeks and finely chop the potatoes and carrots.

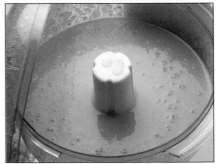

Process the soup in batches in a food processor until smooth.

TORTELLINI VEGETABLE SOUP WITH PISTOU

Preparation time: 30 minutes
Total cooking time: 55 minutes
Serves 6–8

1 tablespoon olive oil
1 leek, finely chopped
1 onion, finely chopped
2 carrots, finely chopped
2 potatoes, finely chopped
2 zucchini, finely chopped
1 stick celery, finely chopped
2 tomatoes, chopped
10 cups (2.5 litres) vegetable stock (see page 83)

375 g (12 oz) tortellini pasta
2 cups (100 g/3¼ oz) basil leaves
3 cloves garlic, chopped
1 cup (100 g/3¼ oz) finely grated Parmesan
5 tablespoons olive oil, extra

1 Heat the oil in a very large pan, add the leek and onion and cook over low heat for 5 minutes, or until just soft. Add the carrot, potato, zucchini and celery and cook over medium heat for 5 minutes, stirring continuously. Add the tomato and stock and bring to the boil. Simmer, covered, over low heat for 20–30 minutes, or until the vegetables are tender.

2 Bring a large saucepan of salted water to the boil and cook the pasta for 6–8 minutes, until *al dente*. Drain, add to the soup and season well.

3 To make the pistou, place the basil in a food processor with the garlic and Parmesan. Process until chopped. With the motor running, add the extra oil. Add a spoonful to each bowl.

NUTRITION PER SERVE (8)
Protein 15 g; Fat 20 g; Carbohydrate 40 g; Dietary Fibre 6 g; Cholesterol 10 mg; 1640 kJ (390 cal)

COOK'S FILE

Serving suggestion: Serve with the Olive oil and garlic griddle breads on page 96.

Add the chopped tomato and stock to the softened vegetables.

Add the al dente (semi-firm) tortellini to the soup.

Process the basil, garlic and Parmesan until finely chopped.

MULLIGATAWNY SOUP

Preparation time: 25 minutes
Total cooking time: 1 hour 25 minutes
Serves 4–6

500 g (1 lb) chicken thigh
　fillets, excess fat removed
2 tablespoons plain flour
1 tablespoon curry powder
1 teaspoon ground turmeric
30 g (1 oz) butter
1 onion, finely chopped
1 apple, peeled, cored and finely
　chopped
 4 cups (1 litre) chicken stock
　(see page 82)

6 whole cloves, tied in muslin
⅓ cup (65 g/2¼ oz) basmati
　rice
1 tablespoon lemon juice
¼ cup (60 ml/2 fl oz) cream

1 Coat the chicken in the combined plain flour, curry powder and turmeric. Heat half the butter in a large pan and cook the chicken over medium heat for 3–4 minutes, or until lightly browned; turn frequently. Remove from the pan and drain on paper towels.
2 Add the remaining butter to the pan, then add the onion, apple and remaining flour mixture and cook for 3 minutes, or until soft. Return the

chicken to the pan along with the stock and cloves. Bring to the boil, reduce the heat and simmer, covered, for 1 hour. Add the rice during the last 15 minutes and cook until it is tender.
3 Remove the chicken; allow to cool slightly and chop finely. Remove the cloves and skim any oil from the surface. Return the chicken to the pan. Reheat gently, stir in the lemon juice and cream, but do not allow the soup to boil. Season to taste with salt and freshly ground black pepper.

NUTRITION PER SERVE (6)
Protein 20 g; Fat 10 g; Carbohydrate 10 g; Dietary Fibre 1 g; Cholesterol 70 mg; 920 kJ (220 cal)

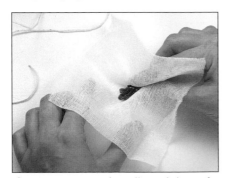

Cut out a square of muslin and tie up the cloves to make a small pouch.

Mix the flour and spices on a plate, and toss in the chicken to coat.

Add the rice to the simmering soup for the last 15 minutes of cooking.

ZUCCHINI CORN CHOWDER

Preparation time: 15 minutes
Total cooking time: 25 minutes
Serves 4

500 g (1 lb) desirée potatoes, diced
1 onion, chopped
2 sticks celery, finely chopped
4 cups (1 litre) chicken stock (see page 82)
1 cup (200 g/6½ oz) corn kernels (either fresh or frozen)
4 zucchini, chopped

1 cup (125 g/4 oz) grated Cheddar
1½ cups (70 g/2¼ oz) roughly chopped rocket leaves
1 cup (250 ml/8 fl oz) milk
4 slices prosciutto, chopped, to serve

1 Place the potato, onion, celery and stock in a large pan and bring to the boil. Simmer, covered, for 20 minutes, or until the vegetables are tender. Leave to cool slightly.
2 Process the vegetables in a food processor until smooth. Return to a clean pan and bring gently to the boil.
3 Reduce the heat, add the corn and zucchini and cook until the zucchini is tender but still firm. Stir in the Cheddar, rocket leaves and milk. Reheat gently, while stirring, but do not allow the soup to boil.
4 Adjust the consistency of the soup with extra stock if necessary. Season to taste with salt and freshly ground black pepper and serve topped with the chopped prosciutto.

NUTRITION PER SERVE
Protein 20 g; Fat 15 g; Carbohydrate 30 g; Dietary Fibre 5 g; Cholesterol 55 mg; 1475 kJ (350 cal)

COOK'S FILE

Serving suggestion: This soup goes very well with the Chilli, corn and red capsicum muffins on page 88.

Using a sharp knife, roughly chop the rocket leaves.

Using a sharp knife, chop the prosciutto into small pieces.

Add the grated Cheddar and rocket leaves to the soup.

Stock

Soup is a dish whose sum is definitely greater than its parts. And one of its most important parts is stock. A good stock makes the difference between an ordinary and a spectacular soup, giving full-bodied flavours and a sound base for the other ingredients. If you are looking at these recipes and thinking the cooking times seeming very long and it all looks like too much trouble, think again. It doesn't take long to chop up the ingredients and then you can leave your stock to simmer lazily while you get on with other things.

BEEF STOCK

Preparation time: 20 minutes
  + refrigeration
Total cooking time: 4 hours 50 minutes
Makes about 7 cups (1.75 litres)

2 kg (4 lb) beef bones
2 unpeeled carrots, chopped
2 unpeeled onions, quartered
2 tablespoons tomato paste
2 sticks celery, leaves included,
  chopped
1 bouquet garni
12 black peppercorns

1 Preheat the oven to hot 210°C (415°F/Gas 6–7). Put the bones in a baking dish and bake for 30 minutes, turning occasionally. Add the carrot and onion and cook for a further 20 minutes. Allow to cool.

2 Put the bones, carrot and onion in a large, heavy-based pan. Drain the excess fat from the baking dish and pour 1 cup (250 ml/8 fl oz) of water into the dish. Stir to dissolve any pan juices; add the liquid to the pan.

3 Add the tomato paste, celery and 10 cups (2.5 litres) water. Bring to the boil, skimming the surface as required and add the bouquet garni and peppercorns. Reduce the heat to low and simmer gently for 4 hours. Skim the froth from the surface regularly.

4 Ladle the stock in batches into a fine sieve sitting over a bowl. Gently press the solids with a ladle to extract all the liquid. Discard the bones and vegetables and set aside to cool. Refrigerate until cold and spoon off any fat that has set on the top. At this stage you can reduce the stock to concentrate its flavour (dilute before using) and store in the refrigerator for up to 2 days or in the freezer for up to 6 months.

CHICKEN STOCK

Preparation time: 20 minutes
  + refrigeration
Total cooking time: 3 hours 10 minutes
Makes about 10 cups (2.5 litres)

2 kg (4 lb) chicken bones
2 unpeeled onions, quartered
2 unpeeled carrots, chopped
2 sticks celery, leaves included,
  chopped
1 bouquet garni
12 black peppercorns

1 Put the chicken bones, onion, carrot, celery and 14 cups (3.5 litres) of water in a large, heavy-based pan. Bring slowly to the boil. Skim the surface as required and add the bouquet garni and peppercorns. Reduce the heat to low and simmer gently for 3 hours. Skim the froth from the surface regularly.

2 Ladle the stock in batches into a fine sieve sitting over a bowl. Gently press the solids with a ladle to extract all the liquid. Let the stock cool, then refrigerate until cold and spoon off any fat that has set on the top. At this stage you can reduce the stock to concentrate its flavour (dilute before using) and store in the refrigerator for up to 2 days or in the freezer for up to 6 months.

FISH STOCK

Preparation time: 20 minutes
+ refrigeration
Total cooking time: 30 minutes
Makes about 7 cups (1.75 litres)

2 kg (4 lb) chopped fish bones,
   heads and tails
1 stick celery, leaves included,
   roughly chopped
1 onion, chopped
1 unpeeled carrot, chopped
1 leek, sliced
1 bouquet garni
12 black peppercorns

1 Place the fish bones, celery, onion, carrot, leek and 8 cups (2 litres) of water in a large, heavy-based pan. Bring slowly to the boil. Skim the surface as required and add the bouquet garni and peppercorns. Reduce the heat to low and simmer very gently for 20 minutes. Skim the froth from the surface regularly.
2 Ladle the stock in batches into a sieve lined with damp muslin sitting over a bowl. To keep a clear fish stock, do not press the solids, but simply allow the stock to strain undisturbed. Allow to cool, then store in the refrigerator for up to 2 days or in the freezer for up to 6 months.

VEGETABLE STOCK

Preparation time: 20 minutes
+ refrigeration
Total cooking time: 1½ hours
Makes about 10 cups (2.5 litres)

1 tablespoon oil
1 onion, chopped
2 leeks, chopped
4 carrots, chopped
2 parsnips, chopped
4 sticks celery, leaves included,
   chopped
2 bay leaves
1 bouquet garni
4 unpeeled cloves garlic
   (see Note)
8 black peppercorns

1 Heat the oil in a large, heavy-based pan and add the onion, leek, carrot, parsnip and celery. Cover and cook for 5 minutes without colouring. Add 12 cups (3 litres) of water. Bring to the boil. Skim the surface if required, and add the bay leaves, bouquet garni, garlic and peppercorns. Reduce the heat to low and simmer for 1 hour. Skim the froth from the surface of the stock regularly.
2 Ladle the stock in batches into a fine sieve sitting over a bowl. Gently press the solids to extract all the liquid.

3 Allow the stock to cool, then refrigerate until cold and spoon off any fat that has set on the top. At this stage you can reduce the stock to concentrate its flavour (dilute before using) and store in the refrigerator for up to 2 days or in the freezer for up to 6 months.
Note: Like a bouquet garni, unpeeled garlic added to a stock adds a subtle flavour and will not cloud the soup.

FREEZING STOCKS

Freezing your stock is useful if you want to prepare ahead. Simply pour the stock into a measuring jug lined with a plastic bag so you can measure how much stock you have and freeze it in convenient portions. Remove the bag from the jug, label the bag, seal securely and freeze.

Alternatively, pour the stock into ice cube trays and freeze. This is useful for fairly concentrated stocks.

BOUQUET GARNI

To make a bouquet garni, wrap the green part of a leek loosely around a bay leaf, sprig of thyme, some celery leaves and a few stalks of parsley, then tie with string. Leave enough string for easy removal.

BREAD

ROSEMARY BREAD TRIOS

Preparation time: 40 minutes
+ 1 hour 40 minutes rising
Total cooking time: 15 minutes
Makes 10 trios

7 g (¹/4 oz) sachet dried yeast
1 teaspoon caster sugar
4 cups (500 g/1 lb) plain flour
1 tablespoon caster sugar, extra
1 teaspoon salt
1 cup (250 ml/8 fl oz) warm milk
¹/4 cup (60 ml/2 fl oz) vegetable oil
10 small sprigs of rosemary
1 egg yolk
sea salt flakes, to sprinkle

1 Combine the yeast, caster sugar and ¹/2 cup (125 ml/4 fl oz) of warm water in a small bowl. Cover and set aside in a warm place for 10 minutes, or until frothy.

2 Sift the flour into a large bowl and stir in the extra caster sugar and salt. Make a well in the centre and pour in the warm milk, oil and frothy yeast. Mix to a soft dough, gather into a ball then turn out onto a lightly floured surface and knead for 10 minutes, or until smooth and elastic. Add a little extra flour if the dough becomes too sticky. Place in a large, oiled bowl, cover loosely with greased plastic wrap and leave in a warm place for 1 hour, or until doubled in size.

3 Punch down the dough, then turn out onto a lightly floured surface and knead for 1 minute. Lightly grease 2 large baking trays. Divide the dough into 10 pieces. Form each piece into three balls—keeping the remaining pieces covered—and place close together on the prepared baking tray; add a sprig of rosemary onto the centre of each trio. Repeat with the remaining pieces of dough, and lay each set separately on the baking tray.

4 Cover the trios with a damp tea towel and set aside for 20 minutes, or until well risen. Preheat the oven to moderate 180°C (350°F/Gas 4). Brush the trios lightly with the combined egg yolk and 1 teaspoon of water and sprinkle with the sea salt flakes. Bake for 15 minutes, or until golden brown. Allow to cool on a wire rack and replace the rosemary sprigs with fresh ones, if you want.

NUTRITION PER TRIO
Protein 7 g; Fat 8 g; Carbohydrate 40 g; Dietary Fibre 2 g; Cholesterol 20 mg; 1080 kJ (260 cal)

COOK'S FILE

Note: 'Punching down' is when you knock the dough with your fist to expel the air.

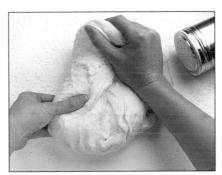

Knead the dough on a lightly floured surface until smooth and elastic.

Arrange the 3 balls together on a lightly greased baking tray.

MINI WHOLEMEAL LOAVES

Preparation time: 40 minutes
  + 2 hours rising
Total cooking time: 45 minutes
Serves 8

15 g (½ oz) fresh yeast
    (or 7 g/¼ oz dried yeast)
1 tablespoon caster sugar
½ cup (125 ml/4 fl oz) warm
    milk
4 cups (600 g /1¼ lb) whole-
    meal plain flour
1 teaspoon salt
¼ cup (60 ml/2 fl oz) oil
1 egg, lightly beaten

1 Grease four 13 x 6½ x 5 cm
(5 x 2¾ x 2 inch) baking tins. Mix the
yeast, sugar and milk in a small bowl.
Cover and set aside in a warm place
until frothy.
2 Combine the flour and salt in a
large bowl. Make a well in the centre
and pour the oil, 1 cup (250 ml/8 fl oz)
of warm water and the frothy yeast
into the well. Mix to a soft dough and
gather into a ball; turn out onto a
floured surface and knead for
10 minutes. Add a little extra flour if
the dough is too sticky. Put in a large
oiled bowl, cover loosely with greased
plastic wrap and leave in a warm
place for 1 hour, or until well risen.
3 Punch down the dough, turn out
onto a floured surface and knead for
1 minute, or until smooth. Divide into
four; knead into shape and put in the
tins. Cover with a damp tea towel and
leave in a warm place for 45 minutes,
or until risen. Preheat the oven to hot
210°C (415°F/Gas 6–7).
4 Brush the loaf tops with the beaten

egg. Bake for 10 minutes, reduce the
temperature to moderate 180°C
(350°F/Gas 4) and bake for a further
30–35 minutes, or until the base
sounds hollow when tapped. Cover
with foil if the tops become too brown.

NUTRITION PER SERVE
Protein 10 g; Fat 10 g; Carbohydrate 40 g;
Dietary Fibre 9 g; Cholesterol 25 mg;
1270 kJ (305 cal)

*Mix the fresh yeast, sugar and milk in a
small bowl until smooth.*

*Gather into a ball and turn out onto a
lightly floured surface.*

*Shape the dough into small loaves and
place in the greased baking tins.*

PARMESAN AND PROSCIUTTO LOAF

Preparation time: 30 minutes
+ 2 hours rising
Total cooking time: 25 minutes
Serves 6

7 g (¹/4 oz) dried yeast
1 teaspoon caster sugar
¹/2 cup (125 ml/4 fl oz) warm
   milk
2 cups (250 g/8 oz) plain flour
1 teaspoon salt
1 egg, lightly beaten
30 g (1 oz) butter, melted and
   cooled slightly
1 tablespoon milk, extra

60 g (2 oz) sliced prosciutto,
   finely chopped
¹/2 cup (35 g/1¹/4 oz) grated
   Parmesan

1 Grease a baking tray. Mix the yeast, sugar and milk in a bowl. Cover and set aside in a warm place for 10 minutes, or until frothy.
2 Mix the flour and salt in a bowl. Make a well in the centre and add the egg, butter and frothy yeast. Mix to a soft dough and gather into a ball; turn out onto a floured surface and knead for 8 minutes, or until elastic.
3 Put in an oiled bowl, cover loosely with greased plastic wrap and leave in a warm place for 1¹/4 hours, or until doubled in size.

4 Punch down the dough, turn out onto a floured surface and knead for 30 seconds, or until smooth. Roll out to a rectangle, 30 x 20 cm (12 x 8 inches), and brush with some extra milk. Sprinkle with the prosciutto and Parmesan, leaving a border. Roll lengthways into a log shape.
5 Lay on the baking tray and brush with the remaining milk. Using a sharp knife, slash the loaf diagonally at intervals. Leave to rise in a warm place for 30 minutes. Preheat the oven to hot 220°C (425°F/Gas 7). Bake the loaf for 25 minutes, or until golden.

NUTRITION PER SERVE
Protein 10 g; Fat 9 g; Carbohydrate 30 g; Dietary Fibre 2 g; Cholesterol 60 mg; 1060 kJ (250 cal)

Sprinkle the prosciutto and Parmesan on the dough, leaving a clear border.

Roll up the dough tightly lengthways into a log shape.

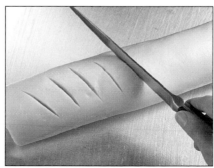

Using a sharp knife, slash the loaf diagonally at intervals.

CHILLI, CORN AND RED CAPSICUM MUFFINS

Preparation time: 15 minutes
Total cooking time: 25 minutes
Makes 12 muffins

1 cup (125 g/4 oz) plain flour
1/4 teaspoon salt
1 tablespoon baking powder
1 cup (150 g/5 oz) polenta
1 tablespoon soft brown sugar
1 egg
1/4 cup (60 ml/2 fl oz) corn oil

2/3 cup (170 ml/51/2 fl oz) milk
   or buttermilk
1 red chilli, finely chopped
1 small red capsicum, finely
   chopped
2 tablespoons chopped basil
   leaves
420 g (131/3 oz) can corn
   kernels, drained

1 Grease twelve 1/2-cup (125 ml/ 4 fl oz) capacity muffin tins. Preheat the oven to moderately hot 200°C (400°F/Gas 6). Sift the flour, salt and baking powder into a bowl and mix in the polenta and sugar. Beat together the egg, oil and milk and add to the dry ingredients. Stir until just moistened, but do not overmix. Add the chilli, capsicum, basil and corn and mix briefly.

2 Spoon the mixture into the muffin tins. Bake for 25 minutes, or until the muffins are well risen. Leave for a few minutes, before turning out onto a wire rack to cool.

NUTRITION PER MUFFIN
Protein 4 g; Fat 6 g; Carbohydrate 25 g; Dietary Fibre 2 g; Cholesterol 20 mg; 730 kJ (175 cal)

Stir the brown sugar and polenta into the sifted flour mixture.

Mix the chilli, capsicum, basil and corn briefly into the flour mixture.

Spoon the mixture into the greased muffin tins.

FOUGASSE

Preparation time: 20 minutes
   + 1 hour 30 minutes rising
Total cooking time: 35 minutes
Serves 4–6

7 g (1/4 oz) dried yeast
1 teaspoon sugar
3 cups (375 g/12 oz) plain
   flour
1 cup (150 g/5 oz) wholemeal
   plain flour
2 teaspoons salt

1 Mix the yeast, sugar and 1/2 cup (125 ml/4 fl oz) of warm water in a bowl. Cover and set aside in a warm place for 10 minutes, or until foamy.

2 Sift the flours and salt, return the husks and make a well in the centre. Pour in 1 cup (250 ml/8 fl oz) of extra warm water and the foamy yeast. Mix to a soft dough and gather into a ball. Turn out onto a floured surface and knead for 10 minutes, or until smooth.

3 Place in a large, lightly oiled bowl, cover loosely with greased plastic wrap and leave in a warm place for 1 hour, or until doubled in size.

4 Punch down the dough and knead for 1 minute. Press into a large, oval shape 2 cm (3/4 inch) thick and make several cuts on either side. Lay on a large, floured baking tray, cover with greased plastic wrap and leave to rise for 20 minutes. Preheat the oven to hot 210°C (415°F/Gas 6–7).

5 Bake for 35 minutes, or until crisp. After 15 minutes, spray with water to make the crust crispy.

NUTRITION PER SERVE (6)
Protein 10 g; Fat 1 g; Carbohydrate 70 g; Dietary Fibre 6 g; Cholesterol 0 mg; 1415 kJ (340 cal)

Leave the yeast mixture in a warm place until well risen and foamy.

Punch down the dough and knead on a floured surface until smooth.

Using a sharp knife, make several slashes on either side of the bread.

Chilli, corn and red capsicum muffins (top) with Fougasse

WHITE DINNER ROLLS

Preparation time: 15 minutes
+ 1 hour 30 minutes rising
Total cooking time: 20 minutes
Makes 12 rolls

1 teaspoon dried yeast
1/2 teaspoon caster sugar
2 cups (250 g/8 oz) plain flour
1/2 teaspoon salt
1 tablespoon dried whole milk
   powder
2 teaspoons caster sugar, extra
1 1/2 tablespoons oil
1 tablespoon milk
poppy seeds, sesame seeds,
   caraway seeds, sea salt
   flakes or plain flour,
   to decorate

1 Combine the yeast, sugar and 1/4 cup (60 ml/2 fl oz) of warm water in a bowl. Cover and set aside in a warm place for 10 minutes, or until frothy.
2 Mix the flour, salt, milk powder and extra sugar in a bowl. Make a well in the centre, and pour in the oil, 1/2 cup (125 ml/4 fl oz) of warm water and the frothy yeast. Mix to a soft dough and knead for 10 minutes, or until smooth and elastic. Add a little extra flour if needed.
3 Place in a lightly oiled bowl, cover loosely with greased plastic wrap and leave in a warm place for 1 hour, or until doubled in size.
4 Punch down, knead for 1 minute and divide into twelve. To shape into spirals, roll each portion into a 30 cm (12 inch) rope, coil tightly and tuck under the end to seal. To shape into knots, tie each rope; or shape into ovals and leave plain or slash diagonally.
5 Place apart on lightly greased trays and cover loosely with a damp tea towel. Leave to rise for 20 minutes. Preheat the oven to moderate 180°C (350°F/Gas 4). Brush with the milk and then sprinkle with your choice of seeds, sea salt flakes or plain flour topping. Bake for 15–20 minutes, or until browned.

NUTRITION PER ROLL
Protein 3 g; Fat 1 g; Carbohydrate 15 g; Dietary Fibre 1 g; Cholesterol 1 mg; 335 kJ (100 cal)

Pour in the oil, warm water and frothy yeast and mix in with a flat-bladed knife.

To make the spirals, coil up the long rope and tuck the end under.

Cover the rolls with a damp tea towel and leave to rise in a warm place.

PUMPKIN DAMPER

Preparation time: 25 minutes
Total cooking time: 25 minutes
Serves 8

1 cup (125 g/4 oz) self-raising
   flour
1½ cups (225 g/7¼ oz)
   wholemeal self-raising flour
1 teaspoon baking powder
1 teaspoon salt
3 tablespoons grated Parmesan
1 egg, lightly beaten
2 teaspoons tomato paste

1 cup (250 g/8 oz) mashed
   pumpkin, well-drained
   (see Note)
3 tablespoons chopped basil
30 g (1 oz) butter, melted
3 tablespoons milk
2 tablespoons pepitas
   (pumpkin seeds)

1 Preheat the oven to hot 210°C (415°F/Gas 6–7). Grease 1 baking tray. Sift the flours, baking powder and salt into a bowl and return the husks. Add the Parmesan and mix in the egg, tomato paste, pumpkin, basil, butter and milk. Mix to a soft dough.

2 Turn out onto a floured surface and knead until smooth. Flatten out to a circle 20 cm (8 inches) in diameter.
3 Place on the baking tray. Using a sharp knife, mark into 8 portions. Brush with water and sprinkle with the pepitas. Bake for 25 minutes, or until cooked through.

NUTRITION PER SERVE
Protein 8 g; Fat 7 g; Carbohydrate 30 g; Dietary Fibre 4 g; Cholesterol 40 mg; 870 kJ (205 cal)

C O O K ' S   F I L E

Note: You will need 400 g (13 oz) of unpeeled raw pumpkin.

Mix together the mashed pumpkin, egg, tomato paste, basil, butter and milk.

Cut through the mixture with a flat-bladed knife until it forms a soft dough.

Using a sharp knife, make deep cuts to form 8 portions.

SAVOURY SCROLL

Preparation time: 35 minutes
Total cooking time: 35 minutes
Serves 6

1 cup (125 g/4 oz) grated
　Cheddar
1/4 cup (25 g/3/4 oz) grated
　Parmesan
1 onion, chopped
1 red capsicum, chopped
100 g (31/4 oz) pancetta,
　chopped
1/4 cup (15 g/1/2 oz) chopped
　parsley
3 cups (375 g/12 oz) self-raising
　flour
1 teaspoon salt
60 g (2 oz) butter, cubed
11/4 cups (315 ml/10 fl oz)
　buttermilk
2 tablespoons olive oil

1 Grease 1 baking tray. Preheat the oven to moderately hot 200°C (400°F/Gas 6). To make the filling, combine the Cheddar, Parmesan, onion, capsicum, pancetta and parsley. Season well with salt and pepper.
2 Sift the flour and salt into a large bowl. Add the butter and rub in with your fingertips until the mixture is crumbly. Make a well in the centre and pour in the buttermilk; mix to a soft dough and gather into a ball. Turn out onto a lightly floured surface and knead until smooth and elastic.
3 Roll out to a 50 x 25 cm (20 x 10 inch) rectangle. Sprinkle the filling over the top, leaving a 2 cm (3/4 inch) border and press the filling down slightly. Roll up lengthways, enclosing the filling. Bring the ends together to form a ring and brush the ends with some water. Press to seal.
4 Place on the prepared tray, snip the outside edge of the scroll with scissors at regular intervals, so the filling is exposed. Bake for 15 minutes, reduce the temperature to moderate 180°C (350°F/Gas 4) and bake for a further 20 minutes, or until golden brown. Brush with the olive oil.

NUTRITION PER SERVE
Protein 20 g; Fat 30 g; Carbohydrate 50 g; Dietary Fibre 3 g; Cholesterol 105 mg; 2195 kJ (525 cal)

Chop the onion and capsicum into small cubes and the pancetta into small pieces.

Using your fingertips, rub the butter into the flour.

Tightly roll up the filled dough lengthways into a log shape.

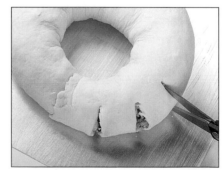

Using sharp scissors, snip the outside edge of the scroll at intervals.

ZUCCHINI AND OLIVE BREAD

Preparation time: 10 minutes
Total cooking time: 40 minutes
Serves 6–8

1 cup (135 g/4½ oz) finely grated zucchini
2 cups (250 g/8 oz) self-raising flour
1 teaspoon baking powder
1 teaspoon salt
1 teaspoon caster sugar
1 cup (125 g/4 oz) grated Cheddar
2 tablespoons chopped chives
12 pitted black olives, sliced
2 eggs
1 cup (250 ml/8 fl oz) milk
3 tablespoons olive oil

1 Preheat the oven to moderately hot 200°C (400°F/Gas 6). Generously grease one 20 x 10 cm (8 x 4 inch) loaf tin.
2 Squeeze as much moisture from the zucchini as possible and set aside.
3 In a large bowl sift the flour, baking powder, salt and sugar. Add the Cheddar, chives and olives. Beat the eggs and add the milk, oil and the zucchini and combine. Make a well in the centre of the dry ingredients and add the zucchini mixture. Stir for 30 seconds, or until well combined.
4 Pour into the prepared tin and bake for 35–40 minutes, or until a skewer inserted comes out clean. Leave to rest for 5 minutes, then turn out onto a wire rack to cool.

NUTRITION PER SERVE (8)
Protein 10 g; Fat 15 g; Carbohydrate 25 g; Dietary Fibre 2 g; Cholesterol 65 mg; 1160 kJ (280 cal)

COOK'S FILE

Hint: The best olives to use are Spanish as Kalamata olives taste a little bitter when cooked.

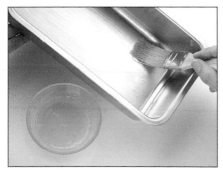

Generously grease the loaf tin with melted butter or oil.

Squeeze the excess moisture from the zucchini over a bowl or the kitchen sink.

Mix in the grated Cheddar, chives and olives to the flour mixture.

RICOTTA AND DILL BUNS

Preparation time: 20 minutes
+ 1 hour 40 minutes rising
Total cooking time: 45 minutes
Makes 8 buns

7 g (¼ oz) dried yeast
1½ tablespoons caster sugar
250 g (8 oz) ricotta cheese
30 g (1 oz) butter, softened
¼ small onion, grated
¼ teaspoon bicarbonate of soda
1 egg
3¾ cups (465 g/14½ oz) plain
    flour
2 tablespoons chopped dill

1 Mix together the yeast, sugar and ¼ cup (60 ml/2 fl oz) of warm water in a bowl. Cover the bowl and set aside in a warm place for 10 minutes, or until frothy.
2 Put the ricotta, butter, onion, bicarbonate of soda and egg in a food processor with 1 teaspoon of salt and process until smooth. Add the frothy yeast and 3 cups (375 g/12 oz) of the flour. Add the remaining flour and mix to a smooth dough. Turn out the dough onto a floured surface and knead for 6–8 minutes, or until smooth. Add the dill during the last minute of kneading.
3 Put in an oiled bowl, cover loosely with greased plastic wrap and set aside for 1 hour, or until doubled in size. Lightly grease one 20 x 30 cm (8 x 12 inch) tray.
4 Punch down the dough and divide into 8 pieces. Form into rounds and lay on the tray. Make 2 slashes on each bun. Cover with a damp tea towel for 30 minutes, or until well risen.
5 Preheat the oven to moderate 180°C (350°F/Gas 4). Bake the buns for 40–45 minutes, or until golden. Check after 20 minutes and reduce the oven to warm 170°C (325°F/Gas 3) if they are too brown.

NUTRITION PER BUN
Protein 10 g; Fat 8 g; Carbohydrate 50 g; Dietary Fibre 2 g; Cholesterol 50 mg; 1250 kJ (300 cal)

Scrape down the sides of the bowl and process the ricotta mixture until smooth.

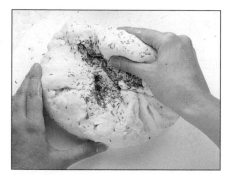

Knead the chopped dill into the dough during the last minute of kneading.

Using a sharp knife, slash the top of each bun twice.

GRISSINI

Preparation time: 40 minutes
  + 30 minutes rising
Total cooking time: 30 minutes
Makes 18 grissini

7 g (1/4 oz) dried yeast
1 tablespoon caster sugar
2/3 cup (170 ml/51/2 fl oz) milk
50 g (13/4 oz) butter
31/2–4 cups (500 g/1 lb) plain
    flour
1 teaspoon salt
sea salt flakes, sesame
    seeds or poppy seeds,
    to decorate

1 Grease 3 baking trays. Mix the yeast, sugar and 1/2 cup (125 ml/4 fl oz) of warm water. Cover and set aside for 10 minutes, or until frothy. In a small pan, heat the milk and butter until the butter has melted.
2 Mix 31/2 cups (435 g/14 oz) of the flour and the salt in a bowl. Make a well in the centre and pour in the milk mixture and frothy yeast. Add enough of the remaining flour to mix to a soft dough, then turn out onto a lightly floured surface and knead for 10 minutes, or until smooth and elastic. Divide into 18 pieces.
3 Roll each piece to the thickness of a pencil and 30 cm (12 inches) in length. Place the grissini 3 cm (11/4 inches)

apart on the baking trays. Cover loosely with greased plastic wrap and leave for 20 minutes.
4 Preheat the oven to hot 210°C (415°F/Gas 6–7). Brush the grissini with cold water and sprinkle with the sea salt or your choice of sesame or poppy seeds. Bake for 15–20 minutes, or until golden brown. Remove from the oven and cool on a wire rack. Reduce the temperature to moderate 180°C (350°F/Gas 4). Return the grissini to the trays, and bake for a further 5–10 minutes, or until crisp.

NUTRITION PER GRISSINO
Protein 3 g; Fat 3 g; Carbohydrate 22 g; Dietary Fibre 1 g; Cholesterol 8 mg; 540 kJ (130 cal)

Heat the milk and butter in a small pan until the butter is melted.

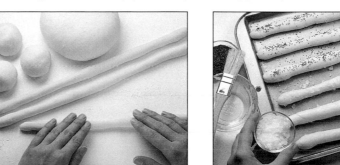

Roll each piece out very thinly on a lightly floured surface.

Brush the grissini with water and add some poppy seeds and sea salt flakes.

OLIVE OIL AND GARLIC GRIDDLE BREADS

Preparation time: 10 minutes
  + 20 minutes + 5 minutes resting
Total cooking time: 20 minutes
Serves 8–10

3¼ cups (400 g/13 oz) plain
  flour
½ teaspoon bicarbonate of soda
½ teaspoon salt
1 teaspoon caster sugar
125 g (4 oz) chilled butter, cut
  into cubes
½ cup (125 ml/4 fl oz)
  buttermilk

1 egg, lightly beaten
2 tablespoons olive oil
2 tablespoons chopped chives
1 clove garlic, crushed
olive oil, for cooking

1 Sift the flour, bicarbonate of soda, salt and sugar. Add the butter and rub in with your fingertips until crumbly. Make a well in the centre and add the buttermilk, egg and oil; stir until the mixture clumps together.
2 Turn out onto a floured surface and knead, gradually incorporating the chives and garlic as you work. Knead for 1 minute, or until you have a uniform, spongy dough.
3 Form into a ball, divide in half and roll out each portion on a floured surface to 7 mm (¾ inch) thick. Using a 6 cm (2½ inch) biscuit cutter, cut out circles and set aside, covered, for 10 minutes. Repeat with the other half.
4 Heat 1 tablespoon of oil in a heavy-based frying pan with a lid. To test the heat of the pan, put a piece of the dough in the pan, cover and fry on one side. Turn it over and brown the other side, uncovered. The dough is cooked when it feels light and hollow. Fry the rest of the dough in batches, adding more oil as needed.

NUTRITION PER SERVE (10)
Protein 6 g; Fat 20 g; Carbohydrate 30 g; Dietary Fibre 2 g; Cholesterol 50 mg; 1250 kJ (300 cal)

On a lightly floured surface, gradually knead in the chives and garlic.

Cut out circles using a biscuit cutter and set aside to allow them to rest.

Fry the breads in batches until browned, light and hollow.

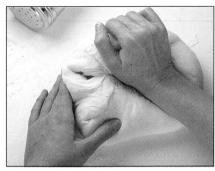

Knead on a lightly floured surface until light and elastic.

Poke your finger into the centre of each ball and make a hole.

Add the bagels to a frying pan of boiling water and boil for 1 minute only.

Sprinkle the top of each bagel with the poppy seeds.

MINI BAGELS

Preparation time: 50 minutes
+ 1 hour 25 minutes rising
Total cooking time: 30 minutes
Makes 22 bagels

15 g (½ oz) fresh yeast
    or 7 g (¼ oz) dried yeast
1 tablespoon sugar
⅔ cup (170 ml/5½ fl oz) warm
    milk
4 cups (500 g/1 lb) plain flour
1 teaspoon salt
30 g (1 oz) butter, melted
1 egg, lightly beaten
1 tablespoon poppy seeds

1 Lightly grease 3 baking trays. Combine the yeast, sugar and milk in a bowl. Cover and set aside in a warm place for 10 minutes, or until frothy. Sift the flour and salt into a large bowl. Make a well in the centre and add the butter, frothy yeast and ⅔ cup (170 ml/5½ fl oz) of warm water. Mix to a soft dough and gather into a ball. Knead for 10 minutes, or until elastic. Place in a lightly oiled bowl, cover loosely with greased plastic wrap and leave for 1 hour, or until doubled in size.

2 Punch down the dough and knead on a well-floured surface until smooth. Divide into 22 pieces. Working with 1 piece at a time (keeping the others covered with a damp tea towel) roll into tight balls. Poke a finger through the centre and gently enlarge the hole until it forms a doughnut. Lay on the baking trays, cover with the tea towel and leave for 10–15 minutes, or until risen.

3 Bring a large frying pan of water to the boil. Add 3–4 bagels at a time and cook for 1 minute. Remove with a slotted spoon and lay on the trays. They will be deflated at this stage.

4 Preheat the oven to moderate 200°C (400°F/Gas 6). Brush the bagels with the egg and sprinkle with the poppy seeds. Bake for 25 minutes, or until browned.

NUTRITION PER BAGEL
Protein 4 g; Fat 2 g; Carbohydrate 20 g;
Dietary Fibre 1 g; Cholesterol 15 mg;
440 kJ (105 cal)

Crostini and Croutons

Crostini (crisp thin slices of baked bread) and croutons (irresistibly crunchy cubes of browned bread) make wonderful accompaniments to any soup, whether it's a broth, creamy soup or chowder.

ROASTED GARLIC CROSTINI

Preheat the oven to moderate 180°C (350°F/Gas 4). Wrap 2 garlic bulbs separately in foil. Bake for 1 hour, or until the garlic feels very soft to touch. Cool. Cut 1 long bread stick diagonally into twenty 2 cm (3/4 inch) thick slices. Lay in a single layer on a large baking tray and brush with 3 tablespoons olive oil. Bake for 10 minutes, or until crisp and golden. Remove any that brown too quickly. Cut the tops off the garlic and squeeze out the flesh. Spread the garlic paste on the bread, sprinkle with a few thyme leaves, salt and freshly ground black pepper. Drizzle on a little extra olive oil, if you want. Serves 4.

NUTRITION PER SERVE
Protein 8 g; Fat 10 g; Carbohydrate 40 g; Dietary Fibre 0 g; Cholesterol 0 mg; 1200 kJ (290 cal)
Note: The garlic becomes very sweet when roasted. Roast an extra garlic bulb if you want more paste.

HERBED CROSTINI FINGERS

Preheat the oven to moderate 180°C (350°F/Gas 4). Combine 80 g (2 3/4 oz) of softened butter with 1 tablespoon each of chopped dill, flat-leaf parsley and basil. Mix until well combined. Stir through 3 tablespoons finely grated Parmesan. Cut 1 long bread stick into diagonal slices, 2 cm (3/4 inch) thick. Spread with the herbed butter. Cut each slice in half lengthways. Place the bread fingers on a baking tray and bake for 10–12 minutes, or until the butter has melted and the edges are crispy. Serves 4.

NUTRITION PER SERVE
Protein 9 g; Fat 20 g; Carbohydrate 36 g; Dietary Fibre 2 g; Cholesterol 60 mg; 1530 kJ (365 cal)

CRISPY CROSTINI

Preheat the oven to moderate 180°C (350°F/Gas 4). Cut half a day old crusty Italian loaf of bread (Ciabatta) into wafer-thin slices. Place the slices in a single layer on a baking tray and brush lightly on one side with a little olive oil. Cook for 8–10 minutes, or until lightly golden. Watch carefully as it is very easy for them to overbrown. Allow to cool. Serves 4.

NUTRITION PER SERVE
Protein 4 g; Fat 15 g; Carbohydrate 25 g; Dietary Fibre 1 g; Cholesterol 0 mg; 1050 kJ (250 cal)

ARTICHOKE AND GARLIC CROSTINI

Preheat the oven to moderate 180°C (350°F/Gas 4). Finely chop 1/4 cup (55 g/2 oz) marinated artichoke hearts and 3 teaspoons capers. Mix with 50 g (1 3/4 oz) softened butter and 2 crushed cloves garlic. Spread the mixture onto 8 thick slices of crusty Italian bread. Cut each slice in half diagonally. Lay on a baking tray and bake for 10–12 minutes, or until the edges are crispy. Serves 4.

NUTRITION PER SERVE
Protein 4 g; Fat 10 g; Carbohydrate 20 g; Dietary Fibre 1 g; Cholesterol 30 mg; 790 kJ (190 cal)

GARLIC AND HERB CROUTONS

Preheat the oven to moderate 180°C (350°F/Gas 4). Cut two 2 cm (3/4 inch) thick slices from a loaf. Remove the crusts and cut each bread slice into 16 cubes. In a bowl, mix together 3 tablespoons olive oil, 2 crushed cloves garlic, 1 tablespoon chopped oregano, 2 teaspoons chopped thyme, 1 teaspoon chopped rosemary and a pinch of chilli flakes. Add the bread cubes to the herbed oil and toss until all the oil has been absorbed. Lay the bread cubes in a single layer on a baking tray and bake in the oven for 10–12 minutes, or until the croutons are golden brown. Turn once during baking. Serves 4.

NUTRITION PER SERVE
Protein 1 g; Fat 15 g; Carbohydrate 7 g; Dietary Fibre 1 g; Cholesterol 0 mg; 690 kJ (165 cal)
Note: Croutons are best made with day-old bread, which holds together better than fresh bread.

PARMESAN TRIANGLE CROUTONS

Preheat the oven to moderate 180°C (350°F/Gas 4). Lightly grease a baking tray. Remove the crusts from 4 slices of bread and cut the slices in half diagonally. Cut each triangle in half and then in half again so that you end up with 8 small triangles. Combine 1/3 cup (80 ml/2 3/4 fl oz) olive oil with 1/3 cup (50 g/1 3/4 oz) finely grated Parmesan. Add the triangles and toss in the mixture. When you add the Parmesan to the oil most of the oil will be absorbed, but you should have enough to coat the triangles. Place the triangles on a lightly greased baking tray. Bake for 10–15 minutes, or until golden. Turn once during baking. Some triangles may be ready before others; if this is the case, remove the golden ones and continue to cook the rest. Serves 4.

NUTRITION PER SERVE
Protein 6 g; Fat 25 g; Carbohydrate 15 g; Dietary Fibre 1 g; Cholesterol 10 mg; 1200 kJ (290 cal)

SPICY CROUTONS

Preheat the oven to moderate 180°C (350°F/Gas 4). Remove the crusts from 4 slices of bread and cut the slices into cubes or, using a small round cutter, cut into circles. Combine 1/4 cup (60 ml/2 fl oz) olive oil, 1 teaspoon each of ground cumin and coriander, 1/2 teaspoon ground cinnamon and a pinch each of ground nutmeg and cloves. Add the bread to the oil and toss until all the oil has been absorbed. Lay the bread in a single layer on a baking tray and bake for 10–15 minutes, or until crisp and golden. Serves 4.

NUTRITION PER SERVE
Protein 1 g; Fat 15 g; Carbohydrate 7 g; Dietary Fibre 0 g; Cholesterol 0 mg; 685 kJ (165 cal)

SUN-DRIED TOMATO AND OLIVE LAVASH BITES

Preheat the oven to moderately hot 190°C (375°F/Gas 5). Soften 40 g (1 1/4 oz) butter and place in a small bowl. Add 2 tablespoons finely chopped sun-dried tomato, 1 tablespoon finely chopped olives, 2 crushed cloves garlic and 2 tablespoons shredded basil. Mix well. Spread the mixture over 1 slice of lavash bread. Cut the lavash into strips then into small triangles. Bake for 5–10 minutes. Watch carefully as they can overbrown quickly. Serves 4.

NUTRITION PER SERVE
Protein 3 g; Fat 8 g; Carbohydrate 12 g; Dietary Fibre 0 g; Cholesterol 25 mg; 590 kJ (140 cal)

ROASTED RED CAPSICUM BUNS

Preparation time: 40 minutes
+ 1 hour 40 minutes rising
Total cooking time: 1 hour
Makes 8 buns

2 red capsicums, cut into large
   flat pieces
7 g (1/4 oz) dried yeast
2 teaspoons sugar
4 cups (500 g/1 lb) plain
   flour
1 teaspoon salt
1 tablespoon olive oil
1 egg, lightly beaten

1 Place the capsicum skin-side-up under a hot grill, until the skins blacken. Cool in a plastic bag, then peel away the skin and cut the capsicum into cubes.
2 Combine the dried yeast, sugar and 1/2 cup (125 ml/4 fl oz) of warm water in a bowl and leave in a warm place for 10 minutes, or until frothy.
3 Sift the flour and salt into a bowl, make a well in the centre and pour in the oil, the frothy yeast and 1 1/4 cups (315 ml/10 fl oz) of warm water. Mix to a soft dough, gather into a ball and knead on a floured surface until smooth. Add a little extra flour if needed. Place in a lightly oiled bowl, cover loosely with greased plastic wrap and leave in a warm place for 1 hour, or until doubled.
4 Punch down the dough, turn out onto a floured surface and knead for 10 minutes, adding the capsicum half way through. Divide the dough into eight and form into rounds. Lay apart on a greased baking tray. Cover with a damp tea towel and leave for 30 minutes, or until well risen. Preheat the oven to moderate 180°C (350°F/ Gas 4). Brush the buns with beaten egg. Bake for 40–45 minutes, or until the base sounds hollow when tapped.

NUTRITION PER BUN
Protein 9 g; Fat 4 g; Carbohydrate 50 g; Dietary Fibre 3 g; Cholesterol 20 mg; 1125 kJ (270 cal)

Sift the flour and salt together into a large bowl.

On a lightly floured surface, knead the dough until smooth.

On a well-floured surface, knead in the capsicum.

WALNUT BREAD

Preparation time: 20 minutes
  + 1 hour 40 minutes rising
Total cooking time: 40 minutes
Serves 8–10

1½ cups (185 g/6 oz) chopped
  walnuts
7 g (¼ oz) dried yeast
1 teaspoon sugar
2 cups (250 g/8 oz) plain flour
1 cup (150 g/5 oz) wholemeal
  plain flour
1 cup (100 g/3½ oz) rye flour
1 teaspoon salt
1 tablespoon plain flour, extra

1 Lay the walnuts on a baking tray and bake in a moderate 180°C (350°F/Gas 4) oven for 5 minutes, or until lightly toasted. Set aside to cool.
2 Mix the yeast, sugar and ½ cup (125 ml/4 fl oz) of warm water in a bowl. Cover and set aside in a warm place for 10 minutes, or until frothy.
3 Combine the flours, salt and walnuts in a large bowl. Make a well in the centre and pour in another 1 cup (250 ml/8 fl oz) of warm water and the frothy yeast. Mix with a flat-bladed knife to a soft dough and gather into a ball. Turn out onto a lightly floured surface and knead for 10 minutes, or until smooth and elastic.

4 Place into a large, lightly oiled bowl, cover loosely with greased plastic wrap and leave for 1 hour, or until slightly risen.
5 Knead for 1 minute. Divide in half and form into 2 rounds 2.5 cm (1 inch) thick. Lay on a floured baking tray and cover with a damp tea towel. Set aside in a warm place for 30 minutes.
6 Sprinkle the top of the loaves with the extra flour by hand or with a sifter. Using a sharp knife, slash the dough diagonally. Bake for 35 minutes, or until crusty and brown.

NUTRITION PER SERVE (10)
Protein 10 g; Fat 10 g; Carbohydrate 40 g; Dietary Fibre 6 g; Cholesterol 0 mg; 1280 kJ (305 cal)

Bake the chopped walnuts on a baking tray until lightly toasted.

Shape each half into a round and place on a lightly floured baking tray.

Sprinkle the loaves with the extra flour by hand or use a sifter.

ONION BUNS

Preparation time: 25 minutes
  + 1 hour 40 minutes rising
Total cooking time: 35 minutes
Makes 12 buns

7 g (¼ oz) dried yeast
1 teaspoon sugar
1 tablespoon olive oil
2 onions, finely chopped
4 cups (500 g/1 lb) plain flour
2 teaspoons salt
1 egg, lightly beaten
1 tablespoon sesame seeds

1 Mix the yeast, sugar and ¹/2 cup (125 ml/4 fl oz) of warm water in a bowl. Cover and set aside in a warm place for 10 minutes, or until frothy. Heat the oil in a frying pan and cook the onion until golden.
2 Sift the flour and salt into a bowl. Stir in the onion and make a well in the centre. Pour in 1 cup (250 ml/ 8 fl oz) of warm water and the yeast. Mix to a soft dough and knead for 10 minutes, or until smooth. Put in an oiled bowl, cover with greased plastic wrap and leave for 1 hour, or until doubled. Grease twelve ¹/2 cup (125 ml/4 fl oz) capacity muffin tins.

3 Punch down the dough, turn out onto a lightly floured surface and knead for 1 minute. Divide the dough into 12 portions and shape each portion into a ball. Place in the tin, cover with a damp tea towel and set aside in a warm place for 30 minutes, or until well risen. Preheat the oven to moderate 180°C (350°F/Gas 4). Brush the buns with the egg and sprinkle with sesame seeds. Bake for 30 minutes, or until crusty.

NUTRITION PER BUN
Protein 6 g; Fat 3 g; Carbohydrate 30 g; Dietary Fibre 2 g; Cholesterol 15 mg; 750 kJ (180 cal)

Cook the finely chopped onion until golden brown.

Place the balls into the large, greased muffin tins.

Brush the buns with the egg and sprinkle with the sesame seeds.

SUNFLOWER BREAD

Preparation time: 10 minutes
Total cooking time: 45 minutes
Serves 6–8

1¼ cups (155 g/5 oz) self-
  raising flour
1 tablespoon caster sugar
2 teaspoons baking powder
1 teaspoon salt
³/4 cup (110 g/3¹/2 oz) fine
  polenta

¹/2 cup (60 g/2 oz) grated Cheddar
2 tablespoons chopped flat-leaf
  parsley
1 teaspoon dried oregano
2 eggs
1 cup (250 ml/8 fl oz) milk
¹/3 cup (80 ml/2³/4 fl oz)
  sunflower oil
2 tablespoons sunflower seeds

1 Preheat the oven to moderate 180°C (350°F/Gas 4). Grease one 20 x 10 cm (8 x 4 inch) loaf tin and line the base with baking paper.

2 Sift the flour, sugar, baking powder and salt into a large bowl. Add the polenta, Cheddar, parsley and oregano. Combine the eggs, milk and oil and pour onto the dry ingredients. Stir until combined.
3 Pour into the tin and sprinkle with the sunflower seeds. Bake for 45 minutes, or until a skewer inserted into the centre comes out clean.

NUTRITION PER SERVE (8)
Protein 8 g; Fat 15 g; Carbohydrate 30 g; Dietary Fibre 1 g; Cholesterol 60 mg; 1215 kJ (290 cal)

Line the base of the greased tin with baking paper.

Add the polenta, Cheddar, parsley and oregano to the bowl and mix.

Sprinkle the sunflower seeds over the top of the bread.

Onion buns (top)
with Sunflower bread

BAKED BUTTERMILK CRISPBREADS

Preparation time: 15 minutes
  + 40 minutes resting
Total cooking time: 1 hour
Makes 12 crispbreads

1 onion, thinly sliced into rings
3$^{1}/_{2}$ teaspoons salt
2$^{2}/_{3}$ cups (335 g/11 oz) plain
    flour
$^{1}/_{2}$ teaspoon bicarbonate of soda
20 g ($^{1}/_{2}$ oz) cold butter, cubed
$^{2}/_{3}$ cup (170 ml/5$^{1}/_{2}$ fl oz)
    buttermilk
4 spring onions, sliced
1 tablespoon finely chopped
    oregano or marjoram
80 g (2$^{3}/_{4}$ oz) butter, melted

1 Put the onion in a colander and sit the colander in a bowl. Sprinkle with 3 teaspoons of the salt. Set aside for 20 minutes, rinse and squeeze dry.

2 Place 2 cups (250 g/8 oz) of the flour, the remaining salt, bicarbonate of soda and butter into a food processor. Blend until crumbly. With the motor running, pour in the buttermilk. Stop processing when the mixture begins to clump together.

3 Transfer to a lightly floured surface and gradually knead in the remaining flour, onion rings, spring onion and oregano or marjoram. You may need a little extra flour. Knead until the dough is almost smooth. Cover with plastic wrap and set aside to rest for 20 minutes.

4 Preheat the oven to moderately hot 200°C (400°F/Gas 6). Divide the dough into 12 portions and working with 1 piece at a time, leave the rest covered. Roll these out thinly on a lightly floured surface to form a circle, about 14 cm (5$^{1}/_{2}$ inches) in diameter.

5 Brush 1 side of each bread with the melted butter and lay on a baking tray, buttered-side-down. Brush with butter. You should fit 3 crispbreads on each tray. Bake for 8–10 minutes, turn over and bake for another 5 minutes, or until golden brown. Repeat with the remaining dough.

NUTRITION PER CRISPBREAD
Protein 4 g; Fat 10 g; Carbohydrate 20 g; Dietary Fibre 1 g; Cholesterol 25 mg; 675 kJ (160 cal)

Sprinkle the sliced onion with salt and sit the colander over a bowl to drain.

Process the dough until the mixture clumps around the blade.

Brush the rolled breads with the melted butter.

Using tongs, turn the browned crispbreads over and bake the other side.

TOMATO HERB ROLLS

Preparation time: 30 minutes
+ 1 hour 35 minutes rising
Total cooking time: 35 minutes
Makes 12 rolls

7 g (1/4 oz) dried yeast
1 teaspoon sugar
4 cups (500 g/l lb) plain flour
1 teaspoon salt
2 cloves garlic, finely chopped
1/2 cup (75 g/2 1/2 oz) sun-dried
   tomatoes, finely chopped
1 tablespoon chopped oregano
1 tablespoon chopped marjoram

1 tablespoon chopped thyme
2 tablespoons chopped flat-leaf
   parsley
30 g (1 oz) butter, melted
1/2 cup (125 ml/4 fl oz) milk,
   plus extra, to glaze

1 Mix the yeast, sugar and 1/2 cup (125 ml/4 fl oz) of warm water in a bowl. Set aside for 10 minutes, or until frothy. Sift the flour and salt into a bowl and make a well in the centre.
2 Mix in the garlic, sun-dried tomato and herbs. Pour in the melted butter, frothy yeast and milk and mix to a soft dough. Knead on a lightly floured surface for 10 minutes, or until

smooth. Cover loosely with greased plastic wrap and leave for 45 minutes, or until well risen.
3 Punch down and knead for 5 minutes. Divide into twelve and roll into balls. Lay apart on a greased baking tray. Leave for 30 minutes, or until well risen. Preheat the oven to hot 210°C (415°F/Gas 6–7). Brush the rolls with milk and bake for 10 minutes. Reduce the oven to 180°C (350°F/Gas 4) and bake for 20–25 minutes, or until golden.

NUTRITION PER ROLL
Protein 5 g; Fat 3 g; Carbohydrate 30 g;
Dietary Fibre 2 g; Cholesterol 8 mg;
730 kJ (175 cal)

Add the garlic, sun-dried tomato and herbs to the flour mixture.

Using a sharp floured knife, divide the dough into 12 equal portions.

The rolls are cooked when the bases sound hollow when tapped.

CHEESE AND HERB PULL-APART LOAF

Preparation time: 25 minutes
+ 1 hour 40 minutes rising
Total cooking time: 30 minutes
Serves 6–8

7 g (¹/4 oz) dried yeast
1 teaspoon sugar
4 cups (500 g/1 lb) plain flour
1¹/2 teaspoons salt
2 tablespoons chopped parsley
2 tablespoons chopped chives
1 tablespoon chopped thyme
60 g (2 oz) Cheddar, grated
milk, to glaze

1 Combine the yeast, sugar and ¹/2 cup (125 ml/4 fl oz) of warm water in a small bowl. Cover and set aside in a warm place for 10 minutes, or until frothy.

2 Sift the flour and salt into a bowl. Make a well in the centre and pour in 1 cup (250 ml/8 fl oz) warm water and the frothy yeast. Mix to a soft dough. Knead on a lightly floured surface for 10 minutes, or until smooth. Put the dough in an oiled bowl, cover loosely with greased plastic wrap and leave for 1 hour, or until doubled in size.

3 Punch down and knead for 1 minute. Divide the dough in half and shape each half into 10 flat discs, 6 cm (2¹/2 inches) in diameter. Mix the fresh

herbs with the Cheddar and put 2 teaspoons on a disc. Press another disc on top. Repeat with the remaining discs and herb mixture.

4 Grease a 21 x 10.5 x 6.5 cm (8¹/2 x 4¹/4 x 2¹/2 inch) loaf tin. Stand the filled discs upright in the prepared tin, squashing them together. Cover the tin with a damp tea towel and set aside in a warm place for 30 minutes, or until well risen. Preheat the oven to hot 210°C (415°F/Gas 6–7).

5 Glaze with a little milk and bake for 30 minutes, or until brown and crusty.

NUTRITION PER SERVE (8)
Protein 10 g; Fat 4 g; Carbohydrate 60 g; Dietary Fibre 3 g; Cholesterol 8 mg; 1255 kJ (300 cal)

Working on a lightly floured surface, flatten the dough into flat discs.

Spoon the filling onto one disc and top with another, pressing down firmly.

Stand the discs upright in the loaf tin, squashing them together.

CARAMELISED ONION BRAIDS

Preparation time: 1 hour
+ 1 hour 35 minutes rising
Total cooking time: 1 hour 35 minutes
Serves 8–10

2½ cups (310 g/10 oz) plain
   flour
1 cup (130 g/4¼ oz) buckwheat
   flour
1 teaspoon salt
15 g (½ oz) fresh yeast or
   7 g (¼ oz) dried yeast
1¼ cups (315 ml/10 fl oz) warm
   milk
30 g (1 oz) butter
1 tablespoon oil
1 kg (2 lb) onions, thinly sliced
   into rings
1 egg, lightly beaten
2 teaspoons fennel seeds

1 Sift the flours and salt into a large bowl and make a well in the centre. Dissolve the yeast in ½ cup (125 ml/4 fl oz) of the warm milk in a small bowl. Then add the remaining warm milk. Pour into the well and mix to a dough. Turn out onto a floured surface and knead for 8 minutes, or until smooth. Place in a large oiled bowl, cover loosely with greased plastic wrap and leave in a warm place for 45 minutes–1 hour, or until doubled in size.

2 Melt the butter and oil in a frying pan, add the onion and cook over medium-low heat for 40–50 minutes, or until the onion is golden.

3 Punch down the dough, turn out onto a lightly floured surface and knead for 10 minutes, or until smooth and elastic.

4 Lightly grease 2 baking trays. Divide the dough in half. Working with 1 piece at a time, divide it into 3 pieces. Roll each piece out to a 30 x 10 cm (12 x 4 inch) rectangle. Divide the onion mixture into 6 portions and spread a portion along the middle of each rectangle, leaving a 2 cm (¾ inch) border. Brush the edge with some of the beaten egg and roll over lengthways to enclose the filling.

5 Plait the 3 pieces together and place seam-side-down on a baking tray. Pinch the ends together. Repeat with the remaining dough and caramelised onion. Cover with a damp tea towel and leave in a warm place for 45 minutes, or until well risen.

6 Preheat the oven to moderate 180°C (350°F/Gas 4). Brush the top with the beaten egg and sprinkle with the fennel seeds. Bake for 35–45 minutes, or until well browned. Transfer to a wire rack to cool.

NUTRITION PER SERVE (10)
Protein 8 g; Fat 7 g; Carbohydrate 40 g; Dietary Fibre 3 g; Cholesterol 30 mg; 1030 kJ (250 cal)

On a lightly floured surface, roll each portion out into a rough rectangle.

Brush the edge with the beaten egg and roll over to enclose the filling.

Plait the 3 pieces together and place seam-side-down on a baking tray.

OLIVE SPIRALS

Preparation time: 25 minutes
  + 1 hour 30 minutes rising
Total cooking time: 35 minutes
Makes 12 spirals

7 g (¹/4 oz) dried yeast
1 teaspoon sugar
4 cups (600 g/1¹/4 lb) plain flour
1 teaspoon salt
2 tablespoons olive oil
2 cups (250 g/8 oz) pitted black
  olives
¹/2 cup (50 g/1³/4 oz) finely
  grated Parmesan
3 cloves garlic, chopped

1 Mix the yeast, sugar and ¹/2 cup (125 ml/4 fl oz) warm water in a bowl. Cover and set aside in a warm place for 10 minutes, or until frothy.
2 Sift the flour and salt into a bowl and make a well in the centre. Add the frothy yeast, oil and 1 cup (250 ml/ 8 fl oz) of warm water. Mix to a soft dough and gather into a ball. Turn out onto a floured surface and knead for 10 minutes, or until smooth. Cover loosely with greased plastic wrap and set aside for 1 hour, or until well risen.
3 Process the olives, Parmesan and garlic in a food processor until chopped. With the motor running, add 1 tablespoon of oil and process to a paste.

4 Punch down the dough and knead for 1 minute. Roll out to a rectangle 42 x 35 cm (18 x 14 inches). Spread with the olive paste, leaving a plain strip along one of the long sides. Roll up lengthways, ending with the plain long side.
5 Cut into 12 slices and place close together on a greased baking tray. Cover with a damp tea towel and set aside for 30 minutes, or until well risen. Preheat the oven to moderately hot 200°C (400°F/Gas 6). Bake for 35 minutes, or until golden brown.

NUTRITION PER SPIRAL
Protein 8 g; Fat 8 g; Carbohydrate 40 g; Dietary Fibre 3 g; Cholesterol 4 mg; 1050 kJ (250 cal)

Spread with olive paste and roll up lengthways.

Using a serrated knife, cut the logs into 12 equal slices.

Place the spirals close together on the baking tray.

SOUR CREAM POLENTA BREAD

Preparation time: 15 minutes
Total cooking time: 50 minutes
Serves 6–8

1½ cups (225 g/7 oz) fine
    polenta
½ cup (60 g/2 oz) plain flour
2 tablespoons soft brown sugar
1 teaspoon baking powder
½ teaspoon bicarbonate
    of soda
½ teaspoon salt
1 egg
⅓ cup (80 ml/2¾ fl oz) milk

1¼ cups (310 g/10 oz) sour
    cream
2 tablespoons vegetable oil
½ teaspoon poppy seeds

1 Preheat the oven to moderately hot 200°C (400°F/Gas 6) and grease one 11 x 18 cm (4½ x 7 inch) loaf tin.
2 Combine the polenta, flour, sugar, baking powder, bicarbonate of soda and salt in a large bowl.
3 Whisk together the egg, milk, sour cream and oil and add them to the dry ingredients, mixing just long enough for them to be evenly combined. Pour the mixture into the tin and sprinkle with the poppy seeds.
4 Bake for 30 minutes, reduce the

temperature to moderate 180°C (350°F/Gas 4) and continue baking for a further 15–20 minutes, or until the loaf is golden.

NUTRITION PER SERVE (8)
Protein 5 g; Fat 20 g; Carbohydrate 30 g; Dietary Fibre 1 g; Cholesterol 70 mg; 1400 kJ (335 cal)

COOK'S FILE

Serving suggestion: Served warm spread with plenty of butter.
Note: There are different grades of polenta; some are finer than others. Compare different brands before purchasing. The fine-textured polenta is best for this recipe as it produces a less coarse bread.

Combine the dry ingredients in a large bowl and mix with a wooden spoon.

Add the combined egg, milk, sour cream and oil and mix until just combined.

Sprinkle the poppy seeds over the top before baking.

BACON, CHEESE AND ONION QUICKBREAD

Preparation time: 25 minutes
Total cooking time: 1 hour 5 minutes
Serves 6–8

1 tablespoon oil
3 onions, thinly sliced into rings
2 teaspoons soft brown sugar
4 rashers bacon, trimmed of
    excess fat and finely chopped
3 cups (375 g/12 oz) self-raising
    flour
100 g (3½ oz) butter, chilled
¾ cup (90 g/3 oz) grated
    Cheddar
½ cup (125 ml/4 fl oz) milk

1 Heat half of the oil in a large, heavy-based frying pan. Add the onion and cook over medium heat for 10 minutes, stirring occasionally. Add the brown sugar and continue to cook for a further 10–15 minutes, or until the onion is golden brown. Set aside to allow to cool. Heat the remaining oil in a small frying pan, add the bacon and cook over moderately high heat until the bacon is crisp. Drain on paper towels and add to the onion mixture.

2 Lightly grease a baking tray. Sift the flour into a large bowl, cut the butter into small cubes and rub into the flour with your fingertips until the mixture resembles breadcrumbs.

3 Add three-quarters of the onion mixture and ½ cup (60 g/2 oz) of the Cheddar to the flour mixture and mix well. Make a well in the centre and add the milk with about ½ cup (125 ml/4 fl oz) of water (add enough water to bring the dough together). Using a flat-bladed knife, mix to a soft dough. Gently knead together to form

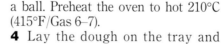
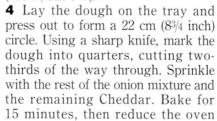
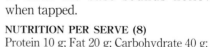

a ball. Preheat the oven to hot 210°C (415°F/Gas 6–7).

4 Lay the dough on the tray and press out to form a 22 cm (8¾ inch) circle. Using a sharp knife, mark the dough into quarters, cutting two-thirds of the way through. Sprinkle with the rest of the onion mixture and the remaining Cheddar. Bake for 15 minutes, then reduce the oven

temperature to moderate 180°C (350°F/Gas 4). Cover the top loosely with foil if it starts getting too brown. Bake for a further 20–25 minutes, or until the base sounds hollow when tapped.

NUTRITION PER SERVE (8)
Protein 10 g; Fat 20 g; Carbohydrate 40 g; Dietary Fibre 2 g; Cholesterol 55 mg; 1525 kJ (365 cal)

Add the onion mixture and some of the Cheddar to the flour and butter mixture.

On a lightly floured surface, knead gently until the mixture forms a ball.

Sprinkle the top with the remaining onion mixture and Cheddar.

INDEX

INTERNATIONAL GLOSSARY OF INGREDIENTS

capsicum	red or green pepper	thick cream	double cream
eggplant	aubergine	cream	single cream
zucchini	courgette	polenta	fine cornmeal
tomato paste (Aus.)	tomato purée, double concentrate (UK)	tomato purée (Aus.)	sieved crushed tomatoes/ passata (UK)

This edition published in 2008 by Bay Books, an imprint of Murdoch Books Limited.
Pier 8/9, 23 Hickson Road, Millers Point NSW 2000, Australia.

Managing Editor: Rachel Carter **Editor:** Pip Vice **Designer:** Wing Ping Tong **Food Director:** Jody Vassallo **Food Editor:** Dimitra Stais **Editorial Assistant:** Faith McKinnon **Photographers:** Joe Filshie, Reg Morrison (step photography) **Food Stylist:** Mary Harris **Food Preparation:** Christine Sheppard **Recipe Development:** Alex Diblasi, Michelle Earl, Joanne Glynn, Barbara Lowery, Kerrie Mullins, Jo Richardson, Tracy Rutherford, Dimitra Stais, Alison Turner **Home Economists:** Anna Beaumont, Michelle Lawton, Kerrie Mullins, Justine Poole, Kerrie Ray, Alison Turner
Chief Executive: Juliet Rogers **Publisher:** Kay Scarlett

The nutritional information provided for each recipe does not include any accompaniments, such as rice, unless they are listed in the ingredients. The values are approximations and can be affected by biological and seasonal variations in food, the unknown composition of some manufactured foods and uncertainty in the dietary database. Nutrient data given are derived primarily from the NUTTAB95 database produced by the Australian New Zealand Food Authority.

ISBN 978 0 68165 771 7
Printed by Hang Tai Printing Company Limited. PRINTED IN CHINA. Reprinted in 2009, 2010.